6-17-75

Creative Divorce
Through Social and
Psychological
Approaches △

Publication Number 943

AMERICAN LECTURE SERIES

A Publication in

The BANNERSTONE DIVISION *of*
AMERICAN LECTURES IN SOCIAL AND
REHABILITATION PSYCHOLOGY

Editors of the Series

JOHN G. CULL, Ph.D.
Director, Regional Counselor Training Program
Department of Rehabilitation Counseling
Virginia Commonwealth University
Fishersville, Virginia

and

RICHARD E. HARDY, Ed.D.
Diplomate in Counseling Psychology (ABPP)
Chairman, Department of Rehabilitation Counseling
Virginia Commonwealth University
Richmond, Virginia

The American Lecture Series in Social and Rehabilitation Psychology offers books which are concerned with man's role in his milieu. Emphasis is placed on how this role can be made more effective in a time of social conflict and a deteriorating physical environment. The books are oriented toward descriptions of what future roles should be and are not concerned exclusively with the delineation and definition of contemporary behavior. Contributors are concerned to a considerable extent with prediction through the use of a functional view of man as opposed to a descriptive, anatomical point of view.

Books in this series are written mainly for the professional practitioner; however, academicians will find them of considerable value in both undergraduate and graduate courses in the helping services.

Creative Divorce Through Social and Psychological Approaches

△

RICHARD E. HARDY
JOHN G. CULL

CHARLES C THOMAS • PUBLISHER
Springfield • Illinois • U.S.A.

Published and Distributed Throughout the World by
CHARLES C THOMAS · PUBLISHER
Bannerstone House
301-327 East Lawrence Avenue, Springfield, Illinois U.S.A.

© *1974 by* CHARLES C THOMAS · PUBLISHER

ISBN 0-398-03101-0

Library of Congress Catalog Card Number: 73-21978

With THOMAS BOOKS *careful attention is given to all details of manufacturing and design. It is the Publisher's desire to present books that are satisfactory as to their physical qualities and artistic possibilities and appropriate for their particular use.* THOMAS BOOKS *will be true to those laws of quality that assure a good name and good will.*

Printed in the United States of America
Y-2

Library of Congress Cataloging in Publication Data

Creative divorce through social and psychological approaches.
Hardy, Richard E.

(American lecture series, publication No. 943. A publication in the Bannerstone division of American lectures in social and rehabilitation psychology)

1. Divorce—United States—Addresses, essays, lectures. 2. Marriage counseling—Addresses, essays, lectures. I. Cull, John G., joint author. II. Title. [DNLM: 1. Divorce. HQ834 C912 1974]

HQ834.H35	362.8'2	73-21978
ISBN 0-398-03101-0		

To Tom and Kay Allan
of Maryland
warm friends and companions

CONTRIBUTORS

Charles Ansell, Ed.D.: Dr. Ansell received his Doctorate at Teachers College, Columbia University. Additionally he received psychoanalytic training from the National Psychological Association for Psychoanalysis where he studied under Theodore Reik. Dr. Ansell, a qualified analyst, has been in continuous private practice as a psychologist and marriage and family counselor in Sherman Oaks, California, since 1960. He is past president of the Los Angeles County Psychological Association; Editor of the California State Psychological Association Newsletter and President of the California State Psychological Association; a frequent lecturer in special programs at UCLA, state colleges and psychiatric hospital staffs, and is consultant to various institutions and social agencies.

John G. Cull, Ph.D.: Professor and Director, Regional Counselor Training Program, Department of Rehabilitation Counseling, Virginia Commonwealth University, Fishersville, Virginia; Adjunct Professor of Psychology and Education, School of General Studies, University of Virginia, Charlottesville, Virginia; Technical Consultant, Rehabilitation Services Administration, United States Department of Health, Education and Welfare, Washington, D.C.; Editor, American Lecture Series in Social and Rehabilitation Psychology, Charles C Thomas, Publisher; Lecturer, Medical Department, Woodrow Wilson Rehabilitation Center; formerly, Rehabilitation Counselor, Texas State Commission for the Blind; Rehabilitation Counselor, Texas Rehabilitation Commission; Director, Division of Research and Program Development, Virginia State Department of Vocational Rehabilitation. The following are some of the books which Dr. Cull has co-authored and co-edited: *Drug Dependence and Rehabilitation Approaches, Fundamentals of Criminal Behavior and Correctional Systems, Rehabilitation of the Drug Abuser with Delinquent Behavior,* and *Therapeutic Needs of the Family.* Dr. Cull has contributed more than sixty publications to the professional literature in psychology and rehabilitation.

Richard E. Hardy, Ed.D.: Diplomate in Counseling Psychology (ABPP); Professor and Chairman, Department of Rehabilitation Counseling, Virginia Commonwealth University, Richmond, Virginia; Technical Consultant, United States Department of Health, Education and Welfare, Rehabilitation Services Administration, Washington, D.C.; Editor, American Lecture Series in Social and Rehabilitation Psychology, Charles C Thomas, Publisher; and Associate Editor, *Journal of Voluntary Action Research*; formerly Rehabilitation Counselor in Virginia; Rehabilitation Advisor, Rehabilitation Services Administration, United States Department of Health, Education and Welfare, Washington, D.C.; former Chief Psychologist and Supervisor of Professional Training, South Carolina Department of Rehabilitation and member of the South Carolina State Board of Examiners in Psychology. The following are some of the books which Dr. Hardy has co-authored and co-edited: *Drug Dependence and Rehabilitation Approaches, Fundamentals of Criminal Behavior and Correctional Systems, Rehabilitation of the Drug Abuser with Delinquent Behavior,* and *Therapeutic Needs of the Family.* Dr. Hardy has contributed more than sixty publications to the professional literature in psychology and rehabilitation.

Peter N. Mayfield, Ph.D.: Dr. Mayfield is a diplomate of the American Board of Professional Psychology with a speciality in clinical psychology. He has been a practicing psychotherapist in Atlanta, Georgia, for ten years. He is a past president of the Georgia Psychological Association.

John A. Scott, Ph.D.: Dr. Scott is in private practice of psychology and marital counseling in Memphis, Tennessee. Dr. Scott also is associated with the Harding Graduate School.

Alberto C. Serrano, M.D.: Director, Community Guidance Center of Bexar County, Texas; Clinical Professor of Psychiatry and Pediatrics and Director, Child and Adolescent Psychiatry, University of Texas Health Science Center at San Antonio.

Marjorie Kawin Toomim, Ph.D.: Dr. Toomim received her Doctorate from the University of Southern California. She has held several positions of responsibility in the Los Angeles area. Currently Dr. Toomim is in private practice. Her areas of interests are in child development, humanistic psychology and individual, group and family counseling.

Helen C. Zusne, Ph.D.: Dr. Zusne received her B.A. degree from Michigan State University and her M.S. and Ph.D. with majors in Clinical Psychology from Purdue University. Her clinical experience includes work at a state neuropsychiatric hospital, a child guidance clinic and a day treatment center. Currently she is in Tulsa, Oklahoma, in private practice which consists of family and marriage counseling, and psychotherapy with children and adults.

PREFACE

More than 1,500,000 people will be divorced and another 1,500,000 will take some steps toward divorce in 1973. These are indeed profound statistics which have implications for millions of adults and children as well as far-reaching financial implications. These figures reflect almost four times the number of divorces which took place only ten years ago. Nearly two out of three divorces today involve children and one in every five remarriages ends in divorce. In the United States 15,000,000 persons now have been divorced.

American attitudes particularly related to sex and a waning family life, more flexible divorce laws and the new independence of the working wife are some of the many factors related to increased divorce. The most divorce prone group are those individuals who are now in their 20's—the post-World War II babies.

Divorce rates are higher in the cities than in rural areas. The smaller the family income and the lower the education the greater the likelihood of divorce. Nonwhites get divorced more frequently than whites.

The financial and emotional implications of divorce can be most profound. For individuals who do not have the financial base of some stability, the sudden economic cost of divorce can be almost staggering. Full understanding of these factors and others can be of great help to marital counselors in their work with clients attempting to adjust to divorce.

We are in debt to the contributors for without them these materials could have never been developed. We wish to express our deepest appreciation to each of them who tolerated our constant letters, calls, negative and positive criticisms.

Richard E. Hardy
John G. Cull

The following books have appeared thus far in The Social and Rehabilitation Psychology Series:

VOCATIONAL REHABILITATION: PROFESSION AND PROCESS
John G. Cull and Richard E. Hardy

CONTEMPORARY FIELD WORK PRACTICES IN REHABILITATION
John G. Cull and Craig R. Colvin

SOCIAL AND REHABILITATION SERVICES FOR THE BLIND
Richard E. Hardy and John G. Cull

FUNDAMENTALS OF CRIMINAL BEHAVIOR AND CORRECTIONAL SYSTEMS
John G. Cull and Richard E. Hardy

MEDICAL AND PSYCHOLOGICAL ASPECTS OF DISABILITY
A. Beatrix Cobb

DRUG DEPENDENCE AND REHABILITATION APPROACHES
Richard E. Hardy and John G. Cull

INTRODUCTION TO CORRECTION REHABILITATION
Richard E. Hardy and John G. Cull

VOLUNTEERISM: AN EMERGING PROFESSION
John G. Cull and Richard E. Hardy

APPLIED VOLUNTEERISM IN COMMUNITY DEVELOPMENT
Richard E. Hardy and John G. Cull

VOCATIONAL EVALUATION FOR REHABILITATION SERVICES
Richard E. Hardy and John G. Cull

ADJUSTMENT TO WORK: A GOAL OF REHABILITATION
John G. Cull and Richard E. Hardy

SPECIAL PROBLEMS IN REHABILITATION
A. Beatrix Cobb

DECIDING ON DIVORCE: PERSONAL AND FAMILY CONSIDERATIONS
John G. Cull and Richard E. Hardy

THERAPEUTIC NEEDS OF THE FAMILY: PROBLEMS, DESCRIPTIONS AND THERAPEUTIC APPROACHES
John G. Cull and Richard E. Hardy

MARITAL AND FAMILY COUNSELING: TECHNIQUES AND APPROACHES
John G. Cull and Richard E. Hardy

CONTENTS

Creative Divorce
Through Social and
Psychological
Approaches

CHAPTER 1

THE ROLE OF THE PSYCHOLOGIST IN ACHIEVING ADJUSTMENT TO DIVORCE

JOHN G. CULL *and* RICHARD E. HARDY

RAPID SOCIAL CHANGE

WHAT IS MARITAL COUNSELING?

INDIVIDUAL ROLE CHANGE

RESPONSIBILITIES OF THE COUNSELOR

F EW COUNSELORS who are concerned in the broad areas of social services including psychiatry, rehabilitation, education, the ministry, social work, and/or psychology can do their work without becoming involved at times with their clients' marital problems. The entire field of marital counseling could be described as a very recent addition to the social service helping field and for this reason there is considerable ambiguity concerning its dimensions and who is qualified to practice.

The marital counselor faces many difficult problems with his clients. He will not give them direct advice concerning what they should do to solve various problems, but he will work with them on a one-to-one basis, in husband-wife sessions and/or in group helping situations in order to explore various approaches to problem solving. The counselor must have considerable information for ready use. This information concerns family stability, feelings, budgets, attitudes, sexual beliefs, marital roles and others.

RAPID SOCIAL CHANGE

Our society is experiencing so much change at such a fast pace that adjustment to change itself is becoming a social problem. This rapid social change which includes, of course, attitudes of all of us concerning moral values, ethics and family behavior is changing life in America and throughout much of the world. Institutions such as the church, the family, governmental structures of service, the university and other educational systems are changing so rapidly that many persons are losing their anchor points for emotional stability. People look around them and find little or no certainty in their jobs, their family life, or the traditional and religious beliefs formerly held sacrosanct.

All of us are deeply influenced by the effects of the mass media such as television. These media depict to us what the outside world seems to be doing. In many cases persons outside of our world seem to be involved in much more exciting activities. Many people live vicariously and some people wish to change their life patterns and family structure in order to relieve boredom and go "where the action is." This immature approach to achieving one's personal goals seldom brings happiness.

With an increased amount of leisure time and a deemphasis on full work days and work weeks, many persons are finding difficulty in managing their personal lives. The changing social environment in which we live has forced the marital counselor into a role of increased importance as a social service professional. His responsibilities affect individuals, their families, work, leisure enjoyment and hopes for personal stability.

WHAT IS MARITAL COUNSELING?

Counseling has been defined in various terms and by many experts. Gustad (1953) has written that "Counseling is a learning oriented process, carried on in a simple, one-to-one social environment in which a counselor, professionally competent in relative psychological skills and knowledge, seeks to assist the client to learn more about himself, to know how to put understanding into effect in relation to clearly perceived, realistically defined goals to the end that the client may be a happier and more productive member of his society."

While definitions vary according to the orientation of the counselor, certain truisms have resulted from the enormous amount of research concerning the effectiveness of counseling. These will be explained in the following paragraphs.

No matter what particular school or theory of counseling is accepted by the practitioner, the most important factor for determining the outcome of counseling effectiveness is the "personality" of the counselor himself. In other words, whether he counts himself as Rogerian, Ellisonian or eclectic, the personality of the counselor will come through in counseling sessions and affect the outcome to a degree which will determine whether or not the counseling session is effective. Just as teachers can bring about enormous growth and changes in students by modifying their attitudes toward various subject matter, the marital counselor can bring about substantial changes in his clients for better or for worse.

Effective counseling requires certain basic ingredients. As the strength or weakness of these ingredients vary so does the ability of the counselor to be effective with the client. There are three basic prerequisites to effective counseling. First, the counselor must accept the client without imposing conditions for this acceptance. He must be willing to work with the client and become actively involved with him as an individual, no matter what may be the counselee's race, attitudes or mode of life. This is necessary in order for the counselee to gain the knowledge that the counselor as a person wishes to help him with his problems and is not prejudging.

The counselor must be "genuine" in that he must function in a way which indicates to the client that he is being true to his own feelings and to himself. To be otherwise is to present a facade to the client—a false image which will act as a deterrent to a successful relationship. Counselors must avoid artificiality in their relationships. If the counselor hides behind a professional mystique, he may find that the counselee is better at "fooling" him than he is at deceiving the client. The professional worker cannot expect his client to be open, sincere or genuine if he himself does not represent these characteristics well.

In addition, the counselor must have an empathic understanding and feeling vis-à-vis the client. He must make a sincere effort to see the client's problems through the client's eyes, and he must be able to communicate the depth of his understanding.

Marital counseling can be considered a relationship between two or more persons which is conducive to good mental health. Inherent in an effective counseling relationship is the absence of threat. The counselor must remove threat if the client is to grow and be able to solve his problems in an uninhibited manner. Counseling as a relationship is also typified by the types of feelings many of us have for our closest friends. True close friendships are characterized by honest caring, genuine interest and a high level of concern about helping in a time of need. Real friendships often require one person to put aside his own selfish needs in order to listen long enough with enough empathy so that a friend's problem may begin to work itself out in a natural and constructive manner.

Marital counseling services vary according to the needs of the client—not the counselor. Often when a counselee comes to the counselor for help he at first will outline a concern which is not the real problem. The counselor must have considerable flexibility and insight in order to know what is required in each individual situation and the appropriate responses for given situations.

The counselor in a marital session always has the goal of bringing about change in the marital relationship. Marital counseling may be effective in helping clients decide whether or not they can "live" with their situation as it is, in changing that situation without separation, in separating for a period of time, or divorcing. All these alternatives are realistic possibilities for end results in successful marital counseling.

Any solution short of total reconciliation is generally considered by our society as indicative of personal failure. This very fact inhibits many people in their exploration of possibilities other than total reconciliation. Many persons fall in line with society's enforced rules and regulations which have particularly forced many persons in the past to remain in unhappy and maladjusted marital situations. The aspect of going for help to a marital counselor for personal adjustment or to a lawyer in order to discuss legal aspects of separation and divorce is also indicative of personal shortcoming in terms of the attitudes of many persons in the society in general. Relatives, peer persons and groups put enormous pressure on the individuals concerned to go back together at all "costs." This "getting back together" in effect saves the family from what some people think of as "disgrace" and makes both family and friends feel more comfortable. Every counselor must take into consideration and impart to his clients the knowledge that while many friends and relatives wish to help, their first thoughts concern what they would like to see as an end result of the consideration rather than what is necessarily best for the partners in difficulty.

Due to strong societal conformity pressure and the problems which individuals have after threatened or actual separation or divorce, they particularly need counseling. Counseling may be concerned with actual problems or anticipated problems of the separation or divorce and the reaction of the individual to the threatened or terminated marriage; or there may be a combination of both of these problem areas.

INDIVIDUAL ROLE CHANGE

Societal change is now fast paced and affects roles which individuals have in marital situations as they experience various aspects of their lives, develop new interests and grow in maturity. A common myth holds that the well adjusted person in our society is one who experiences many worldly things but does not change. All people change and generally change is for the best in terms of an individual's increased maturity. It is important for husband and wife to discuss the redefining of roles which often come about as each grows, matures, and changes in interests. If such discussions are held on a frank basis many questions concerning changes in sexual behavior, business activities, attitudes concerning the importance of work, family entertaining, housekeeping, etc., can be understood more fully.

Role confusion concerning the wife and mother is now profound. Many women no longer are satisfied in devoting their entire lives to family life. Many feel insecure as they see the marriages of their peers "breaking up" with increased regularity. More and more women wish to be self-supporting and self-sufficient and do not wish to relegate themselves to what has been called "house wifery."

This fact also can readily threaten the male who has carried the image of himself as the total bread earner and in many cases the master of his domain. The husband often can misconceive the working role of the wife as one of competition and one which can be a threat to his marriage due to the many new contexts his wife will experience in her work. Her work and his reaction to it can affect greatly whether or not additional children are added to the family unit.

We cannot overstress the importance of periodically discussing and defining roles during the years of marriage. People are, for instance, now living longer. At one time when the last child left home it was near to the time for both husband and wife to die. Today parents experience a new adjustment period in that life continues for many more years after the children have left home. There has been no societal definition of roles for middle aged and older couples. We are seeing now an increase in the number of persons being divorced once the "nest is empty."

RESPONSIBILITIES OF THE COUNSELOR

The counselor must be certain that confidentiality of the marital counseling relationship is maintained and the client must understand this feeling. This includes the counselor's being involved in possible court testimony, at a later date. The counselor must let it be known to his clients and others that he cannot have an effective counseling relationship if either client feels that he is not completely free in discussing various feelings and experiences. Clients must have a clear sense of security.

Counselors come from all segments of society and represent various ages, races, sexes, and religions. Each of them has experienced a variety of conflicts and problems of the same types which trouble their clients. The difference between the client and the counselor (helper and helpee) is that the client is experiencing difficulty and for the most part, counselors feel that their own handicaps and problems are under control. The counselor must guard against automatic feelings of superiority and should see himself as an individual who also has difficulties and who simply wishes to help another individual work his way through problems.

The counselor must be able to recognize when he should refer clients to other counselors or sources of help. There may be problems of counter-transference which interfere with the counseling relationship. Race, age, sex, and religion almost invariably affect the counseling outcomes. For instance, counselors who are older may be out of touch with some of the problems of the younger generation, or male counselors may not fully understand the emerging role of the female in today's society.

Counselors who have strong religious beliefs may be unable to offer unbiased information and those with racial biases and prejudices may experience difficulties of an obvious nature.

Counselors must be certain that they have received adequate training and supervision. Academic requirements in terms of five or six years of college and at least two degrees should have been completed. Supervision in counseling practice as a part of academic and later training is also most important. Each counselor should continue professional growth by active involvement in appropriate professional organizations (according to his interests and trainings). Examples are the American Psychological Association and the American Association of Marriage and Family Counselors. Ethical codes of conduct of these organizations should be strictly followed.

Again, the counselor must guard against the temptation to play "God." Counselors who generally use directive and authoritation approaches are exposed over and over to rationalizations of their own dictatorial motives.

As indicated earlier the personality of the counselor is the decisive factor in the success or failure of therapeutic activities. Counselors constantly must evaluate their own behavior and attitudes toward their work in general and their clients in particular. The counselor must remember that he is working toward the development of the client's ability to make future satisfactory decisions and to achieve a mature dependability.

REFERENCES

Gustad, J.W.: The definition of counseling. In Berdie, R.F.: *Roles and Relationships in Counseling*. Minneapolis, University of Minnesota Press, 1953.

CHAPTER 2

DEALING WITH INITIAL ISOLATION AND LONELINESS AT THE END OF MARRIAGE

JOHN A. SCOTT

THE INITIAL PHASE OF SEPARATION

DEALING WITH ISOLATION AND LONELINESS

THE MELANCHOLY DESPAIR that can come most intensely from bleak loneliness is impressively pictured in the Bible in I Kings 19. Fleeing for his life, Elijah, the prophet, traveled a long solitary journey into the desolate wilderness of Harah and found there a cave for shelter. Ready to give up and die in the midst of total isolation—even feeling no longer the presence of God—he cried: "I, even I alone, am left . . ."

Many a single man and woman has entoned this same melancholy chant.

Any man or woman contemplating divorce must consider the problem of isolation and loneliness and take this factor into account before a final decision is made, or if the decision for separation or divorce is out of one's hands then be prepared to cope with loneliness.

What a sad commentary on our society that even as we are bulging at the seams and there is increasing concern about overpopulation, the problem of loneliness increases. Forty-five percent of the single, formerly married women in America are single by virtue of divorce—not widowhood or annulment (Emerson, 1900). Singles' apartments advertise clubs and activities for singles; drugs, alcoholism, free sex and other forms of frantic activity are vivid reminders of the tragedy of loneliness in the midst of crowds. It is as Erich Fromm (1956) has warned, "the deepest need of man then is the need to overcome his separateness, to leave the prison of his aloneness. The absolute failure to achieve this aim means insanity . . ."

To anticipate most effectively what emotions one might possibly feel upon separation, one should realize that the emotional reaction can be basically the same to any personal loss of any consequence, whether loss of a spouse by death or divorce, the loss of a job, a part of the body, health or even an ideal. In any of these cases it is possible for one to feel, to some extent, one or more of the following emotions: shock, incomprehension, fear, guilt, anger, blame, despair, pain (mental and/or physical), distress, continual preoccupation with the person separated, disinterestedness in life, loss of patterns of conduct.

It is as Richard Wolff (1970) has observed: since the Renaissance the individual has emerged along with many isolating factors, such as the atomization of society, everything moving toward differentiation, specialization, segregation and stratification. It is no wonder then that intense loneliness may quickly result from the trauma of everyday living.

Loneliness results from the absence of intimacy with a fellow human being. One may have the feeling of loneliness even in the presence of fellow human beings, whether they be members of one's family, friends or strangers. Even when one has some degree of intimacy with relatives or friends, loneliness may set in because of the loss (by death or separation) of one who has been especially close. It is the keen sensitivity to the void which remains after the departure of one who occupied an important place in one's life. From the period of infancy, when there is a definite expressed need for attachment to mother, for the rest of one's life the compulsive need for warm, human relationships is keenly felt. So when we lose a loved one or a close association is severed, loneliness is felt even though there are others present who are loved at that time. It is certainly true then that "no man is an island" and, therefore, because of this interrelationship it is superfluous to call, when one hears the chiming of the funeral bells, "send for whom the bell tolls." "It tolls for thee" because all mankind are so interrelated that when anyone dies we all die a little. In any kind of separation one dies a little and thus the symptoms of loneliness are the symptoms of grief. Isolation and loneliness are not simple emotions. They are complex in that they are interrelated with other emotions and so often result from other emotions.

At one time or another one or more of the aforementioned symptoms will be felt by a person recently separated from a close relationship with another. In the case of separation and divorce this is true most obviously, of course, when a spouse feels jilted and the separation is against his or her will. But even in those cases where a separated spouse says of the mate "good riddance," some of these emotions such as anger, guilt, or fear may be present, to some degree, and certainly a period of readjustment will be taking place.

The aforementioned emotions are most vividly felt as the first phase of response to separation. There is a second phase which is more of a healing nature, and while the same aforementioned emotions may persist off and on into the second phase, by and large the second phase is healing (Magraw, 1972). In the second phase, which will be discussed later, the wound may be looked upon as scabbing over as the healing process begins. In the following pages these two phases will be analyzed in some detail.

THE INITIAL PHASE OF SEPARATION

It is, of course, obvious when one party in a marriage suddenly blurts out to a mate, "I'm suing for divorce" that the initial reaction may be shock or perhaps incomprehension. These feelings may either immediately or later merge into a feeling of anger and/or blame. It may be a surprise to some but even in those cases where the marriage has been deteriorating for some months—and this is clearly recognized by both parties involved—there is some degree of shock after the decree of divorce has been granted. Perhaps it is like an amputation. A diseased limb may have been causing pain for some time and one finally comes to recognize that it must be amputated, but the realization, upon coming out of the anesthesia, that the limb is now gone, is still a shock. It may not be as great a shock as when an announcement first comes suddenly out of the blue, before the operation (separation), but it is still a shock.

It is significant that no matter what the circumstances of the party involved, whether one initiates the action or whether one has resisted the separation action, the fact remains that there is emotional upheaval, and this causes one to feel alone. Most people are going to be prone to ask a series of questions evidencing shock, incomprehension, anger, blame, denial, guilt, or self-examination.

The marriage most likely to end in divorce is one that took place after too short a courtship, possibly both man and woman being immature at the time or under some kind of pressure when they got married. Stresses and strains of the first years of marriage have been theirs. One or more children, formation of friends and contacts, purchase of house and/or furniture, striving for advancement in work, etc., have brought pressure on the couple maybe greater than they could take. At a later period in life there would have been other pressures of equal intensity. At any rate, the relationship shows a greater strain than it can stand and so there is an obvious deterioration. Both may recognize this for a time but feel if they don't talk about it, it will go away. It doesn't. The essential needs of the marriage for love, acceptance, romance, interdependency, self-realization, etc. are not met. Husband or wife, or both, seek consolation elsewhere and in other ways. Finally, one or the other blurts out in a moment of anger the desire for divorce as the only way out.

Following, there may be a time of indecision where they both are forced to reexamine each other. Although this may help for a while, it proves futile. Finally they agree to live apart (either in the same house or in separate dwellings).

At this time the initial emotional reactions already referred to may begin to take place. Husband and wife are asking themselves: "Why did we get married in the first place?" "What happened along the way?" "Where did I go wrong?" "Why did spouse change?" "How much am I to blame?" "How much is spouse to blame?" There may even be physical symptoms at this stage such as insomnia, shortness of breath, indigestion, palpitation of the heart, or even asthma, arthritis, bursitis, ulcerative colitis, etc. On the other hand these symptoms may not come until after the divorce if at all. During the time of separation preceding the divorce the couple may live in such a state of disbelief and incomprehension that they are not fully aware of the reality of separation. Because they do not really believe they will actually be finally divorced, these symptoms do not set in yet. Then the divorce becomes final.

As a usual thing the emotions of anger, guilt, hatred, self-examination, etc. become a reality for the first time or else are greatly intensified. No matter who is at fault, there may be a feeling of rejection by the mate. Loneliness and isolation creep in. Other related emotions that are felt may depend, in part, upon the sex of the spouse.

Emotions Most Prominently Felt by Women

A woman is more prone to feel insecure, mentally, physically and financially; and simply because of a woman's "inferior" and "dependent" role in our society, she will be more sensitive about the feelings of rejection (Goldman, 1969). Even if she is the one who sought the divorce, her mind will go back beyond the divorce to a period earlier in the marriage and capitalize on some feeling of rejection at that time. Whether real or imagined, the feeling is there. Seemingly for the same reason, women are more prone to ask, "How can I win him back?"

It should be pointed out that due to the intensity of feeling in circumstances like these, the parties involved are going to think in patterns that would otherwise be illogical or unreasonable to them. For example, a woman a month earlier may have thought to herself, "It will be good riddance to get a divorce from that philanderer," but now may contemplate throwing herself at her husband in order to get him back.

In a majority of cases, because a woman is granted custody of the children, she has many concerns about them: "How can I be both mother and father to the children?" "How will I care for them at home or financially?" "How can I discipline them properly?" Furthermore, she has to try to consider how the children are taking the divorce and what she can do to compensate. She has to try to remember that she may be prone to get lost "feeling sorry for herself" and then forget the fact that the children are suffering too. In many cases the child cannot understand what has happened and wants to be with the departed parent as well as with the one present. While some mothers have a wholesome attitude toward the child's feelings and thus will not make disparaging remarks about the father, other wives try to get even with the father by telling their own side to the children. Also she may try to buy the child's affections with money or favors to buoy a flagging ego.

The loss of self-esteem as a "woman" sets in. As one divorcee put it: "It does something damaging to try and try and try and end up in failure. For two years I did everything possible to save my marriage and it still failed." There is the fear of having to start all over again as a lone female and having to be attractive to men . . . what men? Where are they? How can she attract a man without being "forward" or aggressive? There is also some confusion in her mind about selecting another husband. Because of the emotional turmoil some women are prone to get married too quickly—"on the rebound"—and make another mistake. Other women, in such fear of a second mistake, are too cautious and picky and consequently find no one to suit their high standards.

Divorced women have the problem of realigning their past friendships. Wives with whom they previously played bridge may now be afraid to have their husbands around the divorcee and so, for this and other reasons, her sphere of activities is now curtailed. This is senseless and unfair but often true. In other cases associations with old friends may be too painful without the husband. Different women react in a different way.

Then, of course, there are the practical problems of having to have the time to care for the children and supplement the income as well. Then what about care of the house, appliances, yard or car, or other responsibilities that are typically men's? All of these factors lead to further confusion of her role as a woman. Many other similar details need to be taken into consideration.

A permeating thought in all of this is expressed to oneself: "You have to prove to yourself you are still a person capable of being loved by someone." The feeling of being rejected is so painful you keep asking, "Is it I? What did I do wrong?"

Emotions Peculiar to the Divorced Male

The feeling of inadequacy or dependency upon a woman is usually enhanced by buying, planning or preparing some of his own meals, caring for his own clothes and other responsibilities usually cared for by a woman and taken for granted by a man. Generally, though not always, the man is without his children and thus becomes lonely for them. The contrast of living with a wife and children compared to living alone is sometimes shocking.

Unless the man is very well off financially, he may be in a financial strain having to support wife and children, to some degree, under a separate roof. A split-up family cannot live as cheaply apart as they can together. The financial strain very often leads to bitterness and complaining about how the man is always the one who pays the bill when a family breaks up (Goodman, 1961).

Then there is a realignment of friends as well. Instead of a "couples relationship," it now becomes primarily a relationship with men unless he begins dating again soon. Like his female counterpart, the male may have a shattered ego as a husband and thus he becomes, to some degree, confused over his role as a male. There are other characteristics which vary with the individual personality and circumstances but the man's behavior may often result in compulsive remarriage, flings of all types and/or irrational activity.

Emotions Common to Both Man and Woman Who Are Divorced

To some degree or another, there will be hostility toward the opposite sex. Although this hostility will not necessarily prevent one from dating, it may affect the kind of relationship one has if one dates. It may be cold and distant or on the other hand it may be a passive-aggressive relationship, "using" the opposite sex for personal gratification. The male may be vengeful by being sexually aggressive; the female may show her vengeance by letting a male show her good times on dates or by accepting gifts but without allowing any emotional involvement or commitment on her part.

There is constant concern about the children, no matter which parent they are with. This, naturally, involves worry about how they are taking the separation, and whether their image of husband or wife will have permanent, harmful effects.

With regard to sex, if there was previously a good sex life, the sudden cessation is going to produce sexual tension in which case both are going to be thinking about extramarital sexual activity. It is probably because of loneliness that the majority of divorced women have coitus within one year of divorce. Furthermore, the women who have post-marital coitus report having orgasm more often than they did while married (Bohannan, 1970). It is risky to generalize, but this is probably also due to loneliness. In other cases, depending on the circumstances, one may be revolted by the whole idea of sex due to the circumstances of the dissolved marriage.

Guilt—whether real or imagined—is going to pop up, to some degree, concerning the marriage, its deterioration, divorce, treatment of the children, etc. In many homes a divorce is a violation of the religious teaching of husband or wife, or both, and if not for them it will likely be a violation for some of the relatives. Therefore, to some degree, the religious aspects will play a part in one's guilt feelings. The guilt syndrome can be extremely complicated and far-reaching and can affect future marriage possibilities, as well as the relationship with friends, relatives and church.

Relatives do not prevent a sensation of isolation. In the first place, pride prevents telling them the whole story. In second place, because of their bias, one cannot fully trust their counsel, and because of their emotions they will express extreme views. Then if one lives with relatives it usually isn't long before there are strained relationships. Further, the divorced person does not want to hurt the parents. Thus, very often the relationship with parents, relatives and in-laws becomes confused and indefinite. A divorce is usually embarrassing to the in-laws, as well as the parties involved, and occasionally produces conflicts of various sorts. On the other hand there are cases where parents or relatives are pleased with the divorce. Circumstances vary, but to say the least there is some degree of awkwardness, or at most, total rejection by people who previously have been considered a part of the family circle. An event as traumatic as divorce is rarely without any consequence to relatives. The mother of one divorced man who lived in another city had still not told anyone of her son's divorce after six years.

How can any couple get a divorce without some sense of "failure." Failure in marriage makes one more conscious of failure. Failure always brings on a feeling of isolation, as if to say, "others are successful—I have failed." This is why "misery loves company." One is prone to be more self-conscious about failure in relationships with children or at work or in association with the opposite sex. This makes you more tense and more apt to fail.

A more elusive factor is that emotional conflicts which may have been latent for a long time within the personality of the divorced persons may now be brought into full bloom, having been precipitated by the strain of divorce. These conflicts could be of any kind or to any degree, depending upon one's past. This is something of an unknown factor which the average couple is not in position to predict but even if no deep and serious emotional conflict comes to the surface, the fact remains that divorce is traumatic enough to cause immediate problems as a direct result of this action.

Summary and Example

One may be prone to think that the aforegoing description is not necessarily related to loneliness and isolation, but all of the aforementioned feelings lead into and contribute to loneliness and isolation. Indeed, many of these feelings are a part of loneliness. A person who has these feelings is made more lonely and a person who is lonely is going to find these feelings intensified. It is a vicious cycle and is all a part of the first phase of the reaction to divorce. A person may stay in this first phase only a few days, many months, or permanently, depending upon their personality and background, as well as their circumstances. We all know of recluses who, because of disappointment in love, have remained "in solitary." Usually this phase comes to an end, and as it does so there is a tapering off of the intensity of these feelings, even though they will persist in coming and going for a time.

Take the case of Mrs. A. more than five years before the divorce actually took place there was a crisis in the family and some deterioration of the marriage relationship took place at that time. A change in locality and a change of the man's employment strengthened the family ties and the crisis passed. However, within a few years, a gradual estrangement developed. Three children were involved. The oldest one, having married and left home, was more or less out of the picture but a teenage boy and girl were at home. Off and on the wife sought counseling but the husband never co-operated beyond a couple of visits. The husband took to drinking more heavily and seemed unconcerned about whether the children saw him in an inebriated condition or not. He even offered drinks to the children, much to the disappointment of the mother. There was some concern that his business would suffer but it apparently did not. It seemed as if the father was doing everything possible to alienate his wife as well as his children from him. There was a change in his behavior in many respects.

The details of the separation are unimportant because the feeling of loneliness and isolation is what I want to illustrate. One would think that when the divorce came the mother and the two remaining children would be lined up in opposition to the father for this is the way it appeared through the declining days of the marriage and a period of separation prior to the granting of the divorce. However, such was not the case. The mother seemingly had done everything possible to create peace, hold the family together, stabilize the children, and put the best foot forward. When husband and wife separated, from the appearance of things, the children took the side of the father. Perhaps this was through pity or trying to help him out or strengthen what appeared to be a weak ego. Loneliness was what the mother keenly felt but isolation was added to this when both children went to live with the father. Although the mother was not trying to keep the children away from the father, neither did she expect to be ostracized by them. To her surprise, she felt that she had not been just divorced from her husband, but she felt divorced from her children as well. This intensified the sense of isolation. Naturally, along with this, she felt a keen sense of failure, inadequacy, insecurity and guilt.

But bitterness and resentment were the strongest initial emotions. These were obvious because she felt that for several years her attentions to the weakening marriage kept her from being the kind of mother she knew she ought to have been, and should have been. In essence, her husband had deprived her of her children in two ways. She had first given attention to him and tried to change to his specifications and thereby neglected her children and their needs. In doing this she did an admirable job of showing strength and maturity. She held on beyond what she ought to have done to preserve the home "at least for the children's sake," if not for her own.

Then, secondly, after the separation, the children went with her husband because mother "was so strong she didn't need us." Of course, the mother felt "you can't win." The very trait needed to survive was the source of her immediate defeat—strength.

Thus, the root feeling was "loneliness" but it was manifested outwardly by "anger and resentment."

In another case where the divorced wife had custody of the children, she, too, felt intense loneliness, even with her children. Her husband had insisted that she file for divorce rather than he. She refused to file for some time hoping for a reconciliation, but it never came.

The husband was so desperate to get the divorce (so he could remarry), he threatened to get false witnesses who would testify to adultery with the wife. Even though there was no basis for this, under such a threat the wife was coerced into taking the initial action and sued for divorce. Her loneliness was intensified even in having three wonderful children with her in a comfortable home, when they said ". . . remember Mama, you got the divorce."

It's rare that anyone "wins" in a divorce action.

DEALING WITH ISOLATION AND LONELINESS

The second phase of the separation experience is the healing phase. In spite of the fact that divorce provokes grief and much other unpleasantness, there is some compensation in that grief nearly always is a biphasic process, the second phase of which is healing. The result can be the return of the psyche to an even keel after the stress period. Once the loss is admitted and one faces up to it realistically, one is in better position to "pick up and carry on." What could be considered the usual course of life and functioning could now be pursued normally.

In marriage counseling, when it becomes apparent to client and counselor that the marriage will end in divorce, it should be recognized that termination of the counseling process is not a foregone conclusion. The counselor should frankly discuss with the clients that they will benefit from further counseling. An analysis of possible emotional reactions such as have been discussed on the previous pages will be helpful; support will be needed; some measure of objectivity will be advantageous in making decisions, etc.

Naturally, one is better able to deal with isolation and loneliness only when the fact of separation is admitted. Healing cannot take place until the divorce is admitted and fully recognized as being a reality. The grief resulting from separation must be worked through. This is done by the counselor's continued encouragement of a frank and honest expression of the loss. As in the case of death, I have found it helpful to describe to the parties involved the feelings they can anticipate and, by probing, help them to express these feelings frankly and fully. Sorrow should be expressed even though one is tempted to hide the sorrow behind a facade of nonchalance because it is difficult to admit any degree of failure or it is embarrassing to let on, even slightly, that one has been jilted. The counselor then may need to probe until sobbing and tears are expressed. Grief should not be hidden behind a smoke-screen of artificial cheer. If it is, neurotic symptoms will appear and loneliness and isolation will become worse. Obviously, the counselor needs to watch for unresolved grief. This will be more prone to take place when one has been so completely dependent on the spouse.

Anger is another emotion that must be dealt with to prevent loneliness from becoming too pronounced. Some people become bound up in prolonged grief because they feel themselves justifiably angry at the spouse. It may very well be that as the marriage was breaking up anger was justified because of mistreatment or abuse of one sort or another. Sometimes such anger is allowed to persist without properly being resolved. When this happens rationalization takes place by which anger becomes the defense against accepting the loss. Signs of this may be a bitter flow of accusations against the spouse. Of course, unresolved grief and anger may be an on-going chronic type of problem or may be a recurring situation. After the divorce there are other crises which open old wounds and bring on afresh the old feelings of grief and anger. Such crises may have to do with finance or health, problems with the children, etc. We should recognize, therefore, that any time grief and anger are not properly resolved they may very well lead to a deeper loneliness.

What has been said in the foregoing paragraphs can also be said about the problem of grief if it is delayed in coming to the surface. A couple may go through a divorce with what appears to be flying colors. The "good riddance" attitude may seem to prevail. Then later, associated with loneliness, grief and anger crop up in an unhealthy and harmful way.

In treating anger, as in grief, the client should be encouraged or even prodded into a full expression and analysis of the anger as the first step in treatment. Accompanying this expression, or soon afterwards, one needs to be encouraged to engage in other activities which will drain off the emotional energy of anger into socially accepted channels (Strecker, 1962). This may be done through work, play, hobbies and establishment of other absorbing interpersonal relationships (Menninger, 1942).

Another step in effective treatment of isolation and loneliness is to help the divorced persons accept their own share of responsibility for the ruptured marriage. Either man or woman or both may be prone to project responsibility on the mate and deny their role in provoking or reacting to the mate. A realistic analysis insofar as it is possible must take place. This honest appraisal will help in a number of ways, one of which is the prevention of loneliness because by such an analysis and recognition, the ego in the end will be strengthened and one will not be as prone to "feel sorry for oneself." Of course, it is not the counselor's aim to try to fix what might be called primary responsibility on one or the other. This could increase the burden of guilt. But it is a rare case in which only one party of a marriage is fully responsible for the breakup. Just as it takes two to make marriage a success, it takes two to tear one down.

The matter of responsibility, of course, is related to the matter of guilt. Helping the divorced person to see responsibility is at one end of the spectrum and preventing the person from feeling too much unresolved guilt is at the other end of the spectrum. Once again, as we have already seen, if these emotions exist to an unhealthy degree they will intensify the feeling of loneliness. The way in which guilt is resolved is, of course, a very complicated procedure, depending upon the nature of the guilt, whether real or neurotic. In my judgment Mowrer (1961) has brought a healthy focus on this subject and I believe, in most cases of unresolved guilt, religious resources should be utilized.

The religious faith of the person involved should be utilized in order to resolve the guilt, and if they have no religious faith it will be to their advantage to develop one. I am aware that many therapists consider the subject of religion like a hot potato and are so prone to shy away from dealing with it that they have frequently left the client at sea. Yet, therapists must deal with other subjects which are highly emotionally charged and this is a very real area of importance to the client (Frankl, 1965). Therefore, something must be said about it. It is a rare religious faith that does not take into account, one way or another, the subject of guilt. While there are some religious practitioners who overdo the subject and take advantage of people's emotions in this area, by and large, religious faith has available to the people a procedure for reckoning with the conscience. What may be called spiritual resources will be a decided advantage to divorced persons in more ways than dealing with guilt.

Whether one uses religious faith or not for dealing with guilt, whatever means the counselor has found most effective will likely have to be used to resolve guilt to prevent the client from sinking deeply in the mire of loneliness.

We come now to the core of the implications of this chapter title, namely dealing directly with isolation and loneliness. It has been necessary to deal with related emotions because if they are not reckoned with, one cannot move directly into the sphere of isolation and loneliness. The counselor must help the divorced persons accept their current condition at which time they may be feeling a greater sense of loneliness because their previous friends are no longer in close contact with them. I have heard the divorced blame their friends for either taking sides or else remaining aloof. Naturally, at a time when one is severing a marriage relationship, they need the comfort and support of friends. They would have this were the partner dead but when it is a divorce the friends may feel awkward and, in their reluctance to take sides, they remain at a distance trying to maintain some objectivity. Of course, if they do take sides, the partner whose side they do not take now considers them enemies rather than friends. Another reason why friends may remain aloof is because they are uncertain as to what to say or how to treat those divorced. When they are used to couples getting together it seems awkward to invite their divorced friend who is now single and the friends may not feel that it is appropriate as yet to ask the divorced to bring a date or to provide one for them. It is a difficult situation and there is not an easy answer. At any rate the counselor, through support therapy, may assist the divorced persons by strengthening the ego so that they may begin to form new relationships with the opposite sex insofar as it is consistent with their ethical and moral beliefs.

The greatest need for the persons at the immediate time of breaking up the marriage is for at least one person who can be strong and objective in supporting them. As we have seen, friends and relatives, due to bias and emotional involvement themselves, are not the best ones to fulfill this role, though they are the most usual ones for it.

The counselor has advantages and disadvantages. The advantages are that he or she, as a trained professional person, can be objective and serve as a sounding board by merely being a shoulder to cry on. By reflecting back to the divorced person their feelings and conflicts, true healing can take place. The counselor can best assist the lonely person by refusing to be a biased alter ego; and at the same time give guidance in making the important decisions which turn up at this point by helping the person get all the facts on both sides of an issue out on the table. This is hard for the untrained counselor to do.

The counselor must continue to listen to the lonely person and encourage him or her to pour forth heartache and grief without permitting himself, as counselor, to sink into despair. If he becomes emotionally involved, he cannot be a strong pillar of support.

The counselor's disadvantage is that he may only be available for an hour or two a week. Perhaps even less, since the divorced may have so much expense at that time that they are reluctant to add more by counselor's fees. They may suffer in silence rather than call.

Here is where the counselor may encourage the divorced to seek the services of a minister or church. Many ministers trained in counseling, are available and willing to give such support. I know of many cases where house calls have been made which have been the salvation of lonely people in a time of stress. A minister may be more readily available for emergency calls or may have interested officers or people in his church who would be willing to "lend a sympathetic ear" and at least be present when one needs to talk.

This need to talk to someone—the need for another's presence occasionally in a lonely house or room—is a pressing need for the newly divorced.

The divorced persons, soon after a divorce, usually have very strong feelings about whether to remarry or not to remarry; whereas one person will say with great emotion, "I'll never get married again," another one will say with equal intensity, "I want to marry again as soon as I can." The counselor must make a thorough analysis of the feelings involved in either of these extreme statements; helping the person to evaluate their needs for companionship with the opposite sex is essential at this stage. The divorced, naturally, need to be made aware of the fact that their emotions are going to swing in more than one direction at a time like this and they must be helped to see that caution is necessary to prevent snap decisions which could have unfortunate, lasting consequences.

A mother with children needs to be keenly aware of the fact that in her quest for a father for the children she may not consider enough other factors in dating and possible remarriage. She may need support or encouragement as she begins to date again. The man may confuse his sexual needs with other emotions to such an extent that he will be too quick to leap into another relationship leading to marriage.

This brings up the subject of readjustment of one's affections and sex life. Obviously, if either man or woman has a hang-up about masturbation, this should be frankly discussed and their doubts put at ease. They are going to have ambivalent feelings about overt heterosexual activity at this time. Of course, what they actually do is going to be determined by their moral and ethical sensibilities. Some studies have indicated that one fourth of divorced persons would be willing to remarry the former spouse and a goodly number, at times, have engaged in intercourse with a former spouse (Goode, 1900). The majority of women whose marriages have ended are said to have coitus within one year after the end of the marriage with the average frequency from about 36 to 73 times a year up to the age of 40. Since there can be a wide variety of sexual expressions, a counselor is going to have to give counsel and guidance in accord with the peculiarities of the person involved.

Once the divorced parties are fully aware that they are going to be having to make new friends, it is obvious that they will need to be conscious of making such preparations and engaging in such actions that they will be acceptable to other individuals or groups. This may involve the counselor's helping the parties to be aware of their appearance, manners, mannerisms, etc., so that they will be most likely to be attractive to the opposite sex or, for that matter, accepted by new groups of friends. It should not be beyond the province of the counselor to encourage the divorced parties, where advisable, to enroll in charm courses, Carnegie courses, or other such self-help groups that may be available to meet the needs of the person involved. This will not only help them with the appearance and behavior they need, but a secondary gain will be in venturing out to make new friends and contacts.

It is also to the advantage of counselor and counselee for the divorced parties to be encouraged to attend church. I have already referred to this under the problem of guilt, but the principle of acceptance is involved here. If the person is accepted by a religious group of people, in addition to helping resolve guilt, it will also help a flagging ego. Furthermore, it will give one a new source of contacts and interpersonal relationships which will be strengthening and encouraging to them.

There are other available sources for interpersonal relationships which may come through community resources. There are various types of day care services and/or private schools which may be available for children. Father substitutes may be available to women with children, like the Big Brother organization, or similar services. I know of one lady who takes her children frequently to a nearby fire station because there are a number of men present who always make over the children. Then she has also referred to "the friendly grocer." Even though the prices are a little higher, she considers it worth it because he pays so much attention to her small daughters. In many larger cities there is an organization called Parents Without Partners which is also available as a source of interpersonal contacts.

The counselor needs to be aware that in encouraging the divorced persons by the above mentioned processes to venture out into the world of interpersonal relationships again that this is going to be related to existential situations. Loss of a spouse usually arouses questions about life's meaning and feelings about the final loss of death. This means that the counselor needs to take up these questions with the client because they are definitely related to loneliness and one will not come out of a private corner of isolation if these issues are not, to some degree, faced and resolved. As far as the counselor is concerned, this may involve Educative Counseling involving the suggestion of books or eliciting from within the counselee his or her own feelings about these subjects and whether they are satisfactory for their position in life.

Conclusion

Naturally, the most obvious way of dealing with isolation and loneliness is to encourage a person to come out of isolation and to be with people with whom one may have warm, friendly relationships but this is easier said than done. Sometimes there are emotional blockades which prevent the person from being able to come out of the corner. These blocks such as guilt, hatred, anger and grief tend to isolate a person from his fellow man. Once these negative aspects are cleared away, it will be possible for the counselor then to pursue the instillation of faith—faith in one's self which is self-confidence and self-assurance, as well as faith in others—hope and love. If one has faith in himself, he will have the inner confidence to be able to venture out. If he has faith in others, he will expect to be able to establish relationships with others. "Hope" will motivate the person because he expects and desires to establish interpersonal relationships and if he has "love" then once the interpersonal relationships become possible they can be cemented into deeper and more meaningful ties through love.

Love, of course, is very complicated and takes on many different forms. Ignace Lepp (1964), in a delightful little book entitled *The Ways of Friendship*, explores the many avenues and possibilities of friendship (or love) which may exist between men and men, women and women or between men and women, as well as between parents and children or master and disciple. The point is that there are many possibilities for establishing friendships at various levels. The role of the counselor is to strengthen the ego to such an extent that a person is motivated to go out and to try the various possibilities available to him or her with establishing friendships. Until such a time as the divorced person can feel inclined to do that, it may be that the counselor is the only friend that the person will have. This means that the counselor must be a warm, loving, accepting person. Naturally, to what extent the counselor is able to play this role depends upon the nature and the feelings of the counselor. He certainly should be prepared to give generously of himself and his time. He should be available to talk to the lonely person at most any time. He should be able to encourage, through various means of Support Therapy, so that the lonely and isolated soul in life's darkest hour may find in the counselor a source of strength and hope and, indeed, a close personal friend. Of course, this opens up the vast realm and controversial world of transference. It goes without saying that if the counselor is dealing with a lonely person of the opposite sex that this could lead to emotional involvements which go beyond what either person might at first anticipate. The counselor, therefore, presumably is mature enough and has sufficient insight to be able to control the relationship in such a way that it will be healthy and strengthening to the divorced party.

It is my opinion, contrary to some instruction I received from psychoanalysts years ago, that the counselor can and should be more than just a distant sounding board. I know this is risky. But the lonely person may have no other person to turn to, and thus is in need, temporarily, of a warm, accepting human being (Dahms, 1972). Who can understand more fully the person's feelings than the counselor who has lived through the lonely experience with so many different people? Who is better able to describe, meaningfully, the possible feelings that the lonely may yet have in store?

The lonely person may accept a cold, distant counselor who sits aloof behind his desk and listens for a fee, because there is no one else. Counselors, too often, become robots who mechanically appear to listen (sometimes drowsily), take notes, look at watches and call time, with a rather cold "I understand," and let it go at that. But some demonstration of greater concern and sincerity is needed by the lonely person. This may come by the tone of voice, by verbal expressions or by a hand on the arm or shoulder—perhaps even a phone call between visits, to show a genuine concern. The lonely person is a fellow human who is caught in a miserable storm and for months or years afterward, when the clouds of despair have drifted away, he or she will be filled with gratitude for your warm, human, personal response. But even though this is a precarious situation when dealing with the opposite sex, the counselor can remain in control. This may simply be done at times by a frank statement to the person that his concern must not be interpreted as a romantic interest, that ethics are involved which are vitally important to him.

The responsibility of the counselor in dealing with the naked soul, exposed as it is after coming through divorce action, is a very grave one; he may either save or damn the person, according to the skill with which he fulfills his profession.

REFERENCES

Bohannan, Paul: *Divorce and After.* Garden City, Doubleday, 1970.

Dahms, Alan M.: *Emotional Intimacy.* Boulder, Colo., Pruett, 1972.

Emerson, James G.: The Church and the divorced woman. *Pastoral Psychology, XVIII, 179:23,* 1900.

Frankl, Viktor E.: *The Doctor and the Soul.* New York, Knopf, 1965.

Fromm, Erich: *The Art of Loving.* New York, Harper and Row, 1956.

Goldman, George D. and Milman, Donald S. (Eds.): *Modern Woman, Her Psychology and Sexuality.* Springfield, Ill., Thomas, 1969.

Goode, W.J.: Problems in postdivorce adjustment. *Am Sociol Rev, XIV:* 394-401, 1900.

Goodman, David: The torment of the divorced man. *Coronet, 00:52-56,* 1961.

Lepp, Ignace: *The Ways of Friendship.* New York, Macmillan, 1964.

Magraw, Richard M.: Grief—its clinical importance and its resolution. *Mod Med, 00:62,* 1972.

Menninger, Karl: *Love Against Hate.* New York, Harcourt, Brace & World, 1942.

Mowrer, O. Hobart: *The Crisis in Psychiatry and Religion.* New York, D. Van Nostrand, 1961.

Strecker, Edward: *Understanding Ourselves.* New York, Macmillan, 1962.

Wolff, Richard: *The Meaning of Loneliness.* Wheaton, Ill., Key, 1970.

CHAPTER 3

SUCCESSFUL ADJUSTMENT TO NEW LIFE PATTERNS AND INTERPERSONAL RELATIONSHIPS

PETER N. MAYFIELD

ADJUSTMENT IMMEDIATELY FOLLOWING SEPARATION—
WHAT HELPS?

MEANINGFULNESS OF INDIVIDUAL PSYCHOTHERAPY OR
GROUP THERAPY

▲ ▲ ▲ ▲ ▲ ▲ ▲ ▲ ▲ ▲ ▲ ▲ ▲ ▲

IN STRUCTURING a broad outline for this chapter, the Editors sum-
marized by asking for ". . . . in short, what the individual can
expect when confronting the idea of being a single individual for
some period of time while being accustomed to marriage and the
natural social supports which this gives to a person."

In response, I have taken this charge and have sought consultation
from colleagues and patients by means of a short set of open-ended
questions. At the same time, I have explored some of the literature
relevant to the problem. This chapter, thus, is a summary of my
findings, as these might relate to the needs of professional individuals
engaged in marriage counseling.

As a matter of fact, "marriage counseling" is an inappropriate
term to be using here. As a colleague describes it, we shift into
"divorce counseling" when it becomes apparent that "marriage
counseling" is not appropriate. Divorce counseling, then, becomes
the process described by this entire book, and it is a unique specialty
in its own right. Lawyers have traditionally done this divorce counseling, but from the point of view of an advocate rather than a
counselor committed to the common good of all parties concerned.
This is not to decry the legal profession; I am simply making a
statement of fact. A lawyer is first an advocate of his client, and
can only secondarily do counseling of the couple or family.

Yet separation and divorce are not always adversary proceedings
as we know, and often two individuals wish to dissolve their marriage bonds without making accusations or placing blame. In this
instance, a lawyer may be needed to advise on certain legal tech-
nicalities, but would not be needed otherwise. As "no-fault" divorce
laws become more common, I see the need developing for true
divorce counselors, working without prejudice, to help their clients

work through some of the pain of separation as well as some of the practical matters dealt with in this book.

A look at the current literature clearly reveals a growing interest in providing the tools for effective divorce counseling in general, and there is much useful information on adjustment to new inter-personal relationships in particular.

Especially valuable are *Uncoupling—The Art of Coming Apart* (Sheresky and Mannes, 1972), *When Parents Divorce—A New Approach to New Relationships* (Steinzor, 1969), and *The World of the Formerly Married* (Hunt, 1966).

It would be inappropriate here to attempt a general review of each book, but some sharing of the ideas on social relationships expressed in them might be relevant to the purposes of this chapter.

In introducing their section on the "Aftermath," the authors of *Uncoupling* make this statement: "There are no typical divorced people, but there are typical situations faced by them the moment they are divorced . . ." The chapter then proceeds with empathic analysis of these typical situations, and offers some reassuring comment. At the most general level, every divorced person faces the fact that a wholly different life has begun, both inside the person and outside of him, and the universal question is asked, "What do you do with this life, now that—presumably—it is your own?" Sheresky and Mannes go on to speak of the illusion of freedom; however, in the sense that many men compulsively are drawn to the same type of woman they married before, and likewise women often become attracted to men with a character structure akin to the previous husband. The man with strong dominance needs seeks a submissive woman and then becomes enraged at her passivity; the woman with strong maternal needs seeks a weak man and then becomes depressed at having "again" married an alcoholic. "Instead of freedom and growth, the patterns of familiarity and dependence form again; habit prevails and the sense of renewal gradually drains."

Despite this pessimistic statement, the authors do assert that for many people, their dream of happiness does materialize. They reflect the oftseen statement that many second marriages are considerably happier than the first, and point to statistical evidence that second marriages are typically more permanent than are first marriages. There is less turnover in second marriages—and this kind of stability may be a real part of the "dream" of a newly divorced person.

Finally, the authors describe the important role that friends typically play in helping the newly separated or divorced person endure pain and loneliness. Friends can provide that extra measure of love and acceptance when both are badly needed.

Steinzor, in *When Parents Divorce*, deals with many specific problems that divorced parents face in reestablishing social relationships, and especially in dating. A section on parental dating and children is most helpful. In addition, however, Steinzor offers the general advice to the newly divorced person, "Enjoy your freedom!" He points out that the divorced person has a second chance to conquer inhibitions and reduce the anxieties that may have plagued him earlier. "Freed of his marital vows, the divorced person is relieved of the guilt accompanying adultery or an adulterous thought and is free to have what he often did not have before he was married—a series of maturing love affairs . . . Many who successfully remarry say they feel as if they had never been married before: The emptiness of the first marriage served a good purpose in preparing them for the love they had almost believed was impossible for them."

The World of the Formerly Married is written by an experienced science writer, Morton Hunt. He draws his information from interviews, a questionnaire survey, and the published literature on divorce. His chapter entitled "The Novice" describes some of the personal feelings and social situations a newly separated or divorced person may expect to experience. As the authors above, he speaks of the mixed feelings of tragedy and liberation experienced by many. Loneliness, however, is described as an almost universal experience, excruciating at times. He asks, "But were we not all alone before marriage, without feeling like this?" and answers with the insight that married love is an experience that so profoundly influences a person as to make it impossible ever to be what we were before. ". . . Whatever loneliness may mean to the child, the bachelor, the unmarried girl, it means something else to the Formerly Married—an amputation, a dismemberment, an incompleteness where once there was something whole."

Hunt then goes on to a helpful discussion of ways of reacting to loneliness and dealing with it. Again as Sheresky and Mannes, he points to the importance of friends—someone—to be in touch with, by telephone in the middle of the night, or by letter, long and rambling, but most important, by sheer physical presence. There are some pitfalls to be avoided in relating to friends, Hunt warns, but he provides some insight into avoiding these. Realistically, he prepares the newly separated person for the fact that he will lose some of his friends almost at once, those who take his spouse's side, but that he will be gratified by those who choose his side, or neither. Hunt describes other means of coping with loneliness and self-pity, such as self-indulgence or pampering, liquor, a full regimen of activities and scheduled events, and even rushing into a new full-time relationship. ". . . Sometimes the new liaison is a genuine love affair; more often it is a mere act of desperation designed to fend off loneliness at whatever cost."

Hunt goes on to discuss the subculture of the Formerly Married which he asserts exists as a kind of underground network. Within this fraternity, old members recognize new members and there is a kind of comforting support and reassurance available. Other Formerly Marrieds are thought of as "we," and married people as "they."

In a chapter on "The Marketplace," Hunt suggests that most newly separated people are unaware of the varied means by which potential partners may be met. He then describes in detail some conventional methods, some not-so-conventional methods, and finally what he describes as the "Black Market." He evaluates these methods in terms of their usefulness as Formerly Marrieds have found them. For example, introductions by married friends come across as typically disappointing, if not fraught with a risk not otherwise encountered—the risk of an inescapable bad evening. If the two individuals have been introduced by married friends, there is not much way of escaping each other even if incompatibility seems immediately apparent. With other types of encounters at something such as a cocktail party, either party can disengage at any time with no obligation. Hunt also feels that married couples suffer from a certain blindness or bias in judgment in matching unmarried friends and do not really understand what the Formerly Married person is now seeking in the form of a new relationship. Hunt views unmarried friends or other formerly married people as more realistic, less demanding and less inhibiting!

Other findings from Hunt's research will be integrated into the balance of this chapter, in sections on the job as a source of contacts, also church activities, various organizations, clubs, singles bars, and matchmaking agencies.

At this point, we turn to an analysis of some questions I have posed to colleagues and patients who have experienced divorce or been touched by it in their professional lives. Perhaps it is appropriate to say here that the writer (unlike many writers in this field) has not personally experienced divorce in his own marriage, or in that of his family of origin. This poses a type of bias in the sense of not having *really* experienced these problems directly, but perhaps there is a freedom from the kind of unconscious bias in writing which might otherwise come from past personal experiences. I will quote freely from the responses of those who have "been there," to add more emphasis and authenticity to the ideas which I as only an observer have developed.

Bearing in mind the theme of this chapter as being that of successful adjustment to new interpersonal relationships, I have structured several ideas which relate to means of meeting social needs in formerly married individuals. Obviously some of these would apply to any single person. It will be obvious also, that there is a certain social class bias to these discussions, focusing primarily on the middle class, at both the lower and upper ranges. A chapter such as this written for counseling with lower class persons, especially, would involve meanings and perceptions and socioeconomic realities that would be very unique unto themselves and more properly the scope of a book limited to counseling in the lower class.

Following now is a brief discussion of those points on which you as a counselor may want to be informed before moving into divorce counseling.

SOCIAL ADVANTAGES, DISADVANTAGES OF DIFFERENT TYPES OF HOUSING

Here basically we are speaking of the choice between an apartment and a house, with some variations on each. There are obvious social advantages to living in an apartment complex, which has a clubhouse, swimming pool, tennis courts, and the like. Some apartment groups are well-known for specializing in "swinging singles," while others are quieter and provide some greater degree of privacy. Still others are virtually dead from the standpoint of contributing to one's social life. Once a decision has been made in favor of an apartment, it would seem important to make a rational selection of type based on the client's personality, what he thinks he wants, but also what the counselor senses he may need. A somewhat shy, socially awkward client, male or female, may need the added help he would get in making social contacts by living in an active singles apartment group even though initially he may have reservations about this.

Living in a house offers the formerly married adult relatively little in the way of opportunities for meeting others, but if there are children involved a neighborhood is typically to be preferred over apartment living. Of course, a house provides the opportunity for working in the yard, which for some is an absolute necessity, while, for others, yard work may be one of those things they are hoping to get away from in seeking a new lifestyle. Perhaps one compromise is the idea of a condominium which may offer some greater degree of privacy than a typical apartment complex, but on the other hand is built in close proximity to other condominiums which might together face a common swimming pool or tennis courts.

In summary, it would appear that the type of housing best suited for a given individual would have to do with where he is, where he has been, and where he wants to go with his new lifestyle. If in this person's work activities he does not have many opportunities for meeting others, it would seem more important for him to be in a living situation which would have some built-in social opportunities. Similarly, for the individual who encounters a variety of others all day long, the need for a socially active place of residence is less, and in fact a quieter apartment, house, or condominium may offer him the kind of retreat he needs at the end of the day.

MEANINGFULNESS OF LIVING WITH ROOMMATE(S)

The decision regarding roommates is often one of the most difficult faced by a newly divorced person. On the one hand, there is the constant loneliness that must be dealt with whenever the front door is closed and the outside world shut out. On the other hand, to have an incompatible roommate would be traumatic. My own experience has been that people need a period of time for introspection or otherwise to get their head together, and there seems no better way to deal with this existential crisis period than to live alone for at least a short period of time, if even no more than a few weeks. Then once some idea of lifestyle has been worked out, one knows better the type of roommate to seek, or whether to seek one at all. Again, for some people the presence of a roommate is probably not in their best interest if it can possibly be avoided. Just how much to encourage a client to seek a roommate, or to avoid seeking a roommate probably would have something to do with the client's social adjustment, personal security, and the extent to which you as a counselor are attempting to promote growth and change in your client by environmental manipulation. One client might think he prefers to be left alone with his socially introverted lifestyle, but you may sense that with a little help he may be able to overcome his fears and begin enjoying a more active social life. This person then might be encouraged to seek one or more roommates, for the added social activity these additional persons would create. I have at times recommended seeking a roommate as a means of learning more about how to live with another person. Some people are so wounded following rejection by their spouse that some period of time in living with a roommate would offer the chance to rebuild some self-confidence about themselves as a desirable person. Counseling, at this point, with the newly divorced client might take the form of helping him in this new relationship, helping teach him again how to live with another person comfortably.

One respondent discusses some of the advantages and disadvantages of living with roommates as follows:

> Roommates are often useful in arranging double-dates or making new introductions. It is important that lifestyles are similar or freedom of action suffers . . . (Living alone) there is loneliness, but there is also solitude. One becomes the other and not always when wanted.

Perhaps one brief word here might be injected about returning to live with one's parents following divorce. I can think of only a few instances in which this has worked out satisfactorily, typically where the parents themselves are emotionally healthy, and have a healthy adult relationship with their son or daughter. At times it seems almost an absolute necessity for the client to return to his parents, either because of the need for child care arrangements or because of financial problems. Nonetheless, such a move should be viewed as only temporary and plans should be underway immediately for how and when the person might begin to live independently. This seems like very elemental advice to be giving a client but a number of people have blind spots regarding their relationship with their parents and fail to see the growth-inhibiting aspects of returning home again. Often grown siblings or good friends are willing to take your client in temporarily if he will only ask them.

THE IMPORTANCE OF A WORK SETTING IN ENHANCING SOCIAL ADJUSTMENT

My respondents are virtually unanimous in commenting on the importance of their work setting in social adjustment. If your client is not currently employed then there is an excellent opportunity for you to be alert to the social advantages or disadvantages of job opportunities he may be considering. You need to remember that this newly divorced person is more than likely not very well able to sort out what is important and what is not important in some of his decisions, and you can help a great deal by keeping clearly in mind the social adjustment aspects of various work settings. It is usually possible to spot a dead-end job, one in which there will be no flow of new people coming along. Sometimes a job may appear socially adequate; that is, it may be with a large firm, but still once your client has met people in his or her immediate section there may be little opportunity to socialize beyond. The best jobs for our purposes are those which would put the client in touch with many different people in some direct way. Work, in or around a university setting has proven very successful for some; work as an insurance adjustor provides many opportunities; the paramedical professions such as medical technologist, dental hygienist, or nurse often provide the kind of exposure your client may be seeking. One of my favorites is the hotel business which provides a wide range of job opportunities at all skill levels, while at the same time offering opportunities to interact with hotel guests. This is probably best at resort-type hotels where guests will be staying for a week or more.

In summary, certain job settings are definitely better—or worse —than others in enhancing social adjustment, but this does not always meet the eye and especially does it not always meet the client's eye. Certainly, if there is a choice between earning a few more dollars in one setting, but having better social opportunities in another there would seem to be little doubt regarding the direction in which you would encourage your client. And similarly, even though the client may be offered the opportunity to work in a large office area, still once he has met everyone in the area there may be very little turnover. Finally, for those clients who may already be employed at the time of their divorce, I rather strongly advocate examining the social opportunities available, putting this together with how outgoing the client is and what his living situation may be, and move toward counseling a job change if this seems indicated. He might well be able to continue the same type of work but in a different setting, or continue with the same company but in a different area.

MEANINGFULNESS OF SEEKING FURTHER EDUCATION AS A MEANS OF ENHANCING SOCIAL ADJUSTMENT

Here it is difficult to separate from personal growth the contribution education might make to social growth and development. Obviously, however, there are many social opportunities available in almost any school setting, and college especially meets most of the criteria for maximizing the opportunities for social relationships. Of course, it is quite possible for a day student to go straight to class and then straight home from the last class of the day without ever talking with another student informally. In this as in other situations you may think such a setting would be good for your client, there is the essential ingredient of client motivation and courage to reach out. Thus a client may comply with your recommendations for further schooling or a particular type of housing or a particular type of job, but then torpedo the opportunity by being there with his eyes straight ahead and his mouth closed. This is quite possible in a school setting and it is all the more important that you be alert to this possibility and encourage your client to take a few small steps. To be "encouraged" means to have "courage," and you can help your client through use of various counseling techniques designed to help him overcome fears and develop assertiveness.

When we speak of further education this can take many different shapes and forms ranging from the development of a new career or profession to Adult Education courses offered by colleges, YMCA's, and some churches. For clients who are especially intelligent but undereducated for you to suggest and encourage a serious effort toward a new and higher educational goal will also mean that this person will need to come in contact with people with both his intellectual and educational background. I frequently see divorce situations in which incompatibility stems from one partner being superior to the other in intelligence, even though they both may have equivalent educations (be this high school or college), and as time goes on the brighter partner begins to see his spouse as increasingly stupid. This is usually not the case, in fact, but simply the result of one person of superior intelligence trying to live with another person of "only" average or slightly above average intelligence. From simply a statistical point of view the really bright individual is not likely to find very many others of his or her intelligence level in a typical business or living setting. This person needs to enhance the chances for meeting other equally bright people with whom he can communicate effectively, and this is best done, again, where bright people congregate. Similarly, once a certain level of education has been obtained, especially if this is postgraduate or professional, then the person is immediately accepted into social and intellectual circles that previously had been denied him because he was "only" a college graduate. One respondent writes:

> Those who feel insecure about lack of education will be deprived of feeling secure about *any* adjustment or relationship. In that case further schooling *may* enhance one's self-image.

Regarding Adult Education courses there does not seem to be as much agreement about their effectiveness as for example:

> I have tried it but no social yield yet.

Took one non-credit course—class was too big to get to know anyone but I believe a good potential way to find people with similar interests, depending on course subject.

There are even some other rather obvious, but sometimes overlooked, ideas about enhancing social relationships through educational means. For instance, again using as an example the shy or socially wounded client, if you recommend a college where the students are predominantly of the opposite sex from your client, you may increase significantly the amount of attention and social opportunity your client will receive. I am familiar with one situation in which a young man of my acquaintance attended a college which had until very recently been an all girls' college. This was a very shy, introverted young man and once when I had the occasion to visit him at the college in late afternoon, I was puzzled not to find him in his room or in the library. I asked a coed if by chance she happened to know him and she immediately responded with a smile that yes, she knew him and had recently seen him on another part of the campus. I went to that location, and not seeing him asked another coed. Again the same story; she smiled in immediate recognition of the name, and said he was standing right over there watching an intramural ball game. When I finally came upon him he was standing in a mixed group of students obviously quite happy with his newly found social success!

MEANINGFULNESS OF RELIGIOUS INSTITUTIONS IN MEETING SOCIAL NEEDS

Again, as in education, we have a situation in which social opportunities are typically secondary to the purpose of the activity, but nonetheless a realistic part of it. Lots of people attend lots of church services and activities. Furthermore, it is possible to make some determination of the socioeconomic and educational levels of people attending various churches. Some churches are very heterogeneous in this regard, but many others are rather specialized in the sense of being in a socially elite area of the city, or being near a university. Some such as the Unitarian Church typically attract liberal-minded, rather well educated people. Some churches have a very active program for "singles" and a beauty of these programs is their low cost. Again, you as a counselor need to develop some familiarity with the types of churches available and the kinds of programs they offer which would be of interest to your clients. Most churches do not require that one be a member in order to participate in the various programs of the church. Churches have changed a good bit in recent years in an effort to become more relevant to the social and other needs of the communities they serve, and as one respondent writes:

> I would say the average person who has been away from church ten or more years would be surprised (pleasantly) at the changes which have taken place.

This same person lists as one of the most important factors in his own adjustment, the teaching of a Sunday School class. He writes:

> The material we use in this class is very much oriented toward modern day psychology and current theological philosophies . . . Why did this help me? It was an intellectual path toward a better attitude and understanding of life. It has almost nothing to do with a religious feeling or personal relationship with God . . .

A Roman Catholic respondent, on the other hand, writes:

> Unfortunately the R. C. Church tends to look askance on divorce—most social groups are aimed at singles* or marrieds, *not* (oh, horrors!) "Gay divorced." No, my church is the last place to look for help (singles* *means* single).

Another respondent sums up the potentials of religious institutions by writing:

> Helpful—the second best sex was with someone met at church!

Some churches in larger cities offer Sunday School classes or evening courses in social and personal adjustment, which are open to the public. Other churches sponsor weekend trips which are usually available at very low cost. In my city, one religiously affiliated social service agency is currently offering weekly discussion groups for single parents (most of them are divorced), and programs on how to make a good marriage better, parent-training, family life discussion groups, and a group on the mature woman. Obviously the larger the city, the more these kinds of opportunities are going to be available, but for those counselors who may be working in smaller towns, it still may be useful to know of these things in any nearby city. It is not unusual for people within even a 50 to 75-mile radius of a large city to come in and avail themselves of these kinds of activities and of opportunities, even if for no more than a couple of hours.

ROLE OF SPECIAL INTEREST GROUPS IN MEETING SOCIAL NEEDS

There is an amazing array of special interest groups and clubs of all sorts available to the public in larger cities. Many of these groups attract singles especially, and have significant social overtones regardless of the specific purpose of the club. In Atlanta, the Ski Club is probably the most well-known of these, but also there is a Flying Club, Sailing Club, a Wine Tasting Society, an Appalachian Trail Club, a Conservation Club, a Zoological Society, and the newest one, a Retriever Club. There are various cultural and musical groups which meet regularly and offer enjoyment to their participants. If your client attends one of these groups "cold" he needs to be prepared for the fact that for the first few meetings he will definitely feel like an outsider, but that with persistence and regular attendance he can become known to an increasingly larger circle of people there. He may need your encouragement to persist since often it takes a bit of courage to be the stranger in any group. Obviously it would help if he could find a friend to accompany him.

My respondents have a good bit to say about these groups.

If you join a group simply to find "a man" I feel you are doomed to disappointment, but it *is* important to "circulate," to reach outside yourself to enlarge your circle of friends.

The special interest groups possibly bring people together of similar intents. There may be a more respectable aura around them. It does offer the so-called protection of the group as well as the setting for meeting on a social basis. This very well might be the most satisfying path for the person who wants to find friends of similar taste and interests.

In your role as counselor you may wish to acquaint yourself with the various kinds of opportunities available in your area; some naturally gregarious clients will find out these opportunities on their own, but others would never learn of them, but once informed might enjoy participating. This whole area has been referred to as "the joining syndrome" and we can view it both in terms of man's effort to improve himself and his environment, but also as a means of reaching out to others, moving away from loneliness.

One special interest group which has particular significance for the formerly married is Parents Without Partners. This is a national organization with chapters in many towns and cities. Its function is that of enabling single parents "to learn better ways of helping themselves and their children cope with life in the one-parent or divided family." Obviously in addition to this goal, however, P.W.P. offers many social opportunities, at relatively low cost. One chapter in a large city offers weekly dances, "coffee and conversation" at members houses, bridge, camping, skating parties, and picnics.

SINGLES BARS AND MISCELLANEOUS OPPORTUNITIES FOR THE FORMERLY MARRIED

In larger cities certain lounges or bars have developed as meeting places for "singles," where men and women can go unescorted. Typically, these are crowded, there is dancing, and one is free to return home with company or alone as one wishes. My respondents offer a variety of attitudes towards them:

> No experience. Apparently, this is mainly for quick and temporary liaisons.
>
> "Singles" bars probably appeal to the more gregarious. It provides the opportunity for the casual, easy pickup, relationships which rarely develop into lasting ones. Some may be content to have these easy relationships with the come-and-go connotations . . .
>
> I found "singles" bars to be very helpful. Not only did I have the opportunity to meet lots of interesting people of both sexes, but also was "educated" as to the forms of dress, behavior, expectations in dating, and the latest words. When one is going to a singles bar one has to dress well and snap out of feeling blue. Meeting friends there makes it more fun and one feels rather safe.

Singles bars are not unlike large cocktail parties in which there is no obligation to anyone, but if two people happen to hit it off well, they can take it from there. These introductions are usually "cold," however, and the individual involved has to be very much alert to what he or she may be getting into and take things small step by small step, with eyes wide open.

Similar to singles bars with respect to "cold" introductions are the various computer dating services. These are proliferating at a rapid pace and in the classified ads on any typical day in Atlanta there are half-a-dozen different dating services available. Hunt (1966) describes such dating services as being "black market" and there are indeed many risks attendant to them. A main problem here is the lack of assurance of confidentiality regarding information sent in to the "computer." Nonetheless, there is a certain amount of intrigue attached to the possibility that a computer with integrity could find the "right one."

Going still beyond the computer are direct advertisements of oneself and what one is looking for. In a recent nationwide periodical the following "personal" advertisements appear:

Skier, 40, seeks . . . female companion to share Alta, Bugaboos . . .

Man, 35, desires female acquaintances. My interests; social, political, signs of the times . . .

Widow, attractive, well-educated, spirited, late 40's desires companionship of man possessing comparable "joie de vivre" . . .

The various methods described in this section have an appeal and a sense of adventure not unlike that of deep-sea fishing. You drop in your hook and you never know what you are likely to come up with! It is my opinion that there is a lack of excitement and adventure in the lives of many people and it is for this reason, in part, that strangers are willing to take chances on strangers. It is truly a "market place" as Hunt says.

ROLE OF SEX IN DATING PATTERNS—WHAT A "NEWCOMER" MAY EXPECT TODAY

Most of my respondents have an opinion on this subject and I will rely heavily on their observations:

A "newcomer" is in for a shock—particularly a woman who must conform to new permissiveness or stay home. Most are willing conformers, however.

One may expect sex as part of a relationship—after one or several dates in most cases. But, in some, virginity is still alive and well.

Wow! I was shocked to find the husbands of my friends already regard me speculatively as a possible "easy make." They confide their indiscretions to me freely now. I can already foresee that sex will no longer be a matter of choice, but a "modus operandi."

A newcomer could be shocked by the new openness of sex. However, one gets what one asks for, and people usually respect ones wishes. Sex is much freer and has lots less strings attached to it. A new single person shouldn't expect a marriage proposal after sleeping with someone once or twice, or ten times. This new freedom is great, once one gets used to it.

Throughout these remarks there is the idea that liberalization of attitude towards sex is going to be a part of successful adjustment to a new life after marriage. How much of an adjustment is required can be determined to some extent by the age of your client and the extent to which moral values are deeply rooted in religious beliefs. The respondent above who commented that ". . . in some virginity is still alive and well" offers a note of encouragement to those who have strong feelings about adherence to more conventional morality!

SPECIAL PROBLEMS CREATED BY BEING OF A CERTAIN AGE—UNDER TWENTY OR OVER FORTY

In the younger age group, especially if there are no children, adjustment to divorce is usually the easiest. There are many early short-lived marriages which are over before the partners are out of their teens, and typically, these partners revert quickly back to a single state without major adjustment problems. Where a child or children do exist it seems to be fairly typical for the mother and children to return to the mother's natural home where grandparents (again, typically in their forties at this point) can play an active role in child care and child raising. This often enables the young mother to attend college or finish her high school education, and begin circulating again.

In the over-forty age group, my respondents come forth with an interesting variety of comments:

The only problem of being over forty is in your mind. It takes a while to realize there is no problem. Just remember *all* of your contemporaries (there are lots of them) are at the same point, all others soon will be. Any age is strictly a temporary arrangement.

At age 44, I find many girls too young or immature. An age differential of 6 to 15 years seems to work best.

Let's face it, a woman over forty limits herself to male companions who are also over forty, while a man over forty is attractive to almost any age woman. He has limitless chances for any relationship, from casual to intense—not so for an older woman.

Here the men over forty do not seem to be hurting, but women over forty appear to have a different problem since they are thrown in competition with much younger women who may be *physically* more attractive. Perhaps some help for both men and women comes from cosmetic surgery:

> If you have age signs which can be helped by plastic surgery, and can afford it, it is very helpful and can really help you feel great. I think therapists should be aware of possibilities of what can be done, and the feeling it can give one; "a second start" feeling.

ADJUSTMENT IMMEDIATELY FOLLOWING SEPARATION—WHAT HELPS?

It is in attempting to write this section that I feel most helpless, and in turn, most heavily dependent on "those who have been there" for their comments:

> I have found that in periods of total desperation pulling the covers tautly over my head gave temporary relief from the pain of adjusting, but when I emerged, all the mean uglies were still hovering over me. I'm not sure this is a facetious remark. I personally believe that at first there is absolutely nothing that really helps . . . the adjustment period is just something that has to be toughed out. For me adjustment was like having a baby—you're in labor, you can't escape, but suddenly it's over, and somehow miraculously you've made it. There is a point beyond which things, activities, and even people cannot help. You must see it through.

> Learning that it's misery for others too—being able to talk out feelings with friend or therapist. Magazine articles describing the experiences of others help.

> *COMPANY*, just being with people as opposed to being by yourself in an apartment somewhere.

> "Using" my close friends freely, for comfort and support; honest grief and introspection; crowding my days with "business"; *reading!*; remembering that *time heals!*

> The divorcee is fortunate if she has understanding friends . . . sometimes a change of environment can open up new areas of satisfaction. For some, the comfort of the known may be more sustaining.

> New surroundings are the best thing! One is so busy getting settled that there is no time for regrets. Being in a new place, one has to

"get out" and time just flies. Close friends who don't ask questions but are always available can make all the difference in the world.

Obviously, loneliness is the major social problem immediately following separation. There seems to be a normal grief reaction which only the person involved can work out for himself. Once over this, however, a loneliness sets in which affects people in varying degrees and for varying lengths of time. You may wish to acquire a copy of *Conquering Loneliness* (Rosenbaum & Rosenbaum, 1973) for review and recommendation to your clients. This recent book is written by a psychiatrist and his psychologist wife who strive to tell how ". . . you can overcome loneliness and achieve contentment, both in solitude and with others." This book is practical in approach, offering a number of ways for a person to help himself fight his personal battle against loneliness. The authors describe one approach through meditation. Some instruction in meditation is given and the person is encouraged to practice meditation daily: "Once you have made the practice of meditation a habit, setting aside a few minutes each day to purge your mind of pent-up feelings in a state of quietude and relaxation you will grow to look forward to the time each day that you reserve for this purpose, just as you look forward to a good hot shower to refresh you physically after a trying day's work."

MEANINGFULNESS OF INDIVIDUAL PSYCHOTHERAPY OR GROUP THERAPY

As a psychotherapist, I often relate to individuals who are experiencing the break-up and dissolution of their marriage. I share the grief, loneliness, and fear of those I see in the consulting room. I try to be of some help in exploring answers to the inevitable question of "what went wrong?" There is an analysis of new relationships. There is an analysis of the relationship the patient forms with me, a feeling of trust and sharing develops which is often unique to the person's past experience of relationships, and a model grows on which future relationships may be based.

The kind of experience described above is similar to what your client may expect if he enters into a psychotherapy relationship with a qualified, conventional, therapist. I add the term "conventional" to emphasize the fact that today there are several unconventional modes of psychotherapy which may or may not be of help to your client. If you live in an area where you have a choice of a variety of approaches in psychotherapy among local practitioners, I suggest that you know who you are referring to, what his approach is, and give your client some structure before making a referral.

My respondents comment on the meaningfulness of psychotherapy as follows:

> Greatest usefulness was in accepting break-up of marriage and home.
>
> I am utterly committed to therapy as a means of facing reality (seeing oneself and one's environment as it is, not as one wishes it were or pretends it to be). No matter how bitter is the taste of reality, it is infinitely preferable to pretense or a dream world.
>
> Have had both individual and group therapy and consider both invaluable. It is very difficult to describe why and how they are meaningful, even though you recognize it as a powerful and effective tool.
>
> Psychotherapy (individual) may be meaningful on different levels. This I think depends upon the person's motivation. It can offer self-revelation and the opportunity to sort out what caused the marriage breakdown. Also it may give the ego support which the divorcee needs, particularly if there is much self-blame. In addition it may provide the opportunity to grow up—to accept adult responsibility.

Supplementing individual and group psychotherapy as resources for your clients are some other lesser known opportunities. First, the Institute for Advanced Study in Rational Psychotherapy lists in its current series, workshops on "Creative Contacts and Relationships for Single People" instructed by Albert Ellis, Ph.D. These workshops are described as dealing with ". . . some of the frequent blocks to developing interpersonal relationships toward the end of helping participants develop their potential for creative intimacy. Areas to be dealt with will include fear of rejection, developing assertion, competitiveness, overcoming loneliness, and developing sensitivity to others' feelings. The workshop will demonstrate basic techniques for meeting strangers; keeping conversation going; thinking on your feet; and consolidating acquaintances. Psychological homework for continued personal development will be outlined, and, where possible, adapted to individual participants."

Finally, an offering by the Human Development Institute describes their program entitled "Singles Groups" which can be purchased in the form of audio cassettes. These cassettes are used in leaderless groups. This particular program for singles ". . . is a program to help people learn about loving. It was developed especially for single, unattached adults who seek more fulfilling relationships, and deals with such important issues as moving towards another, moving away from another, asking for love, declaring and expressing affection, handling rejection and disappointment, being free to say no, and accepting affection."

Closing Remarks

With all of the foregoing, no matter how well equipped you are as a divorce counselor, you cannot lead your client's life for him once he has left your office. In addition to advice and information, you need to convince your client to act on what you have given him. Counseling can be likened to friendly persuasion. To take steps, to make changes all takes initiative and courage on the part of your client, and you need to give him through your own genuineness and conviction the encouragement he seeks and usually needs.

REFERENCES

Hunt, M.: *The World of the Formerly Married.* New York, McGraw-Hill, 1966.

Human Development Institute: 1973 brochure. Chicago, Illinois.

Institute for Advanced Study in Rational Psychotherapy: 1973 brochure. New York, New York.

Rosenbaum, Jean, M.D. and Rosenbaum, V.: *Conquering Loneliness.* New York, Random House, 1969.

Sheresky, Norman and Mannes, M.: *Uncoupling, the Art of Coming Apart.* New York, The Viking Press, 1972.

Steinzor, Bernard: *When Parents Divorce.* New York, Random House, 1969.

CHAPTER 4

SPECIAL PROBLEMS OF MEN

CHARLES ANSELL

I HAD BEEN TALKING with Fred, a lawyer in his mid-forties. He frequently represented clients in divorce proceedings. Our discussion that day turned to the always delicate question of how we, as professional men, understand our own experiences as husbands, as fathers, and sometimes, as divorced men. Fred was divorced over two years ago, but he was currently involved with a woman whom he regarded more seriously than most.

"When I at last realized that Nancy and I were divorcing after fifteen years as man and wife, I knew I had reached a crisis in my life." He turned his head away for an instant reflecting on some silent thought. "You know," he began, "the Chinese symbol for Crisis is represented by two signs. One reads danger, the other reads opportunity. I had a choice. I took opportunity to resolve my crisis." He smiled widely at his observation. Clearly, Fred had grown since his divorce.

This chapter may well have been titled, not The Special Problems of Men, but The Special Problems of Fred and Alan and Lionel and Donald. Divorced men may encounter similar experiences, but the differences in their views of these experiences would be too wide to reduce to a set of generalizations.

The probability is that Fred and Alan and Lionel and Don will encounter a sudden loneliness in the first days after the separation, but what each of these men will do to ease the loneliness will vary as widely as their basic personalities. Fred may feel such relief at being free of the oppressive climate of his marriage that his aloneness may never turn to loneliness. Lionel, on the other hand, chronically unsure of himself, uncertain of his decisions, fearful that in losing Ellen he had lost all of his potential as a man among women, will proceed to spend his evenings at the telephone calling his old friends to complain tearfully, to strip himself bare emotionally until he reduces his friends to uttering empty banalities. "Pull yourself together Lionel. Lionel it's only temporary. You'll meet other women soon . . ." "But," (Lionel is prepared for all that.) "How did I fail Ellen? How?"

Yet, despite the wide difference in personality between Fred and Lionel in their characteristic ways of living in a crisis, there remain certain obseravtions that statistically at least point to several generalizations about men after divorce. Young men under 25 years of age who marry early and divorce soon after encounter a widely different postdivorce life than men over 34. Younger men, for reasons not relevant here, may unconsciously view their erstwhile marriage as a date stretched out too long. Divorce comes easy. A quick return to dating nurtures the illusion that little of serious consequence has occurred. Divorce to the young does not come often with the ominous feeling of crisis. Perhaps divorce for the young lacks the content of crisis-anxiety which older men find in divorce.

This is not to deny that the young can not know crisis; this is only to aver that the nature of crisis as perceived differ between the under 25 and over 34. It would be tempting to turn aside for the moment to ponder the question of which of the two reactions to divorce is, or should be the "norm"? Should it be the seeming casualness of men under 25, or the often crisis-shaken reaction of men over 34? In either case, the reaction to divorce does not descend as a moral problem with its attendant preoccupations with remorse and guilt. Nor would the crisis which divorce often poses be resolved by a reordering of moral perspectives. Most often, the crisis reaction to divorce carries the special sting of personal failure. For many men failure at a task which they meant to succeed at, indeed which they felt they were expected to succeed at, can drop them to despair. The young man on the other hand may not suffer his divorce in such stark failure terms as he might suffer if he were suddenly terminated mid-way in some special studies leading to a career. The nature of distress felt most acutely by the younger man rises from an abrupt frustration of private fantasies, fantasies more related to his personal conquest of his world than to the fantasies related to self-enrichment through marriage and family.

Again, the crisis of divorce felt by the older man follows upon a marriage that lasted not one or two years but most often ten and fifteen years and more. His marriage produced children whom he fathered from infancy into active young people. He was witness to their problems and their experiences from infancy to adolescence and older. His children entered his life and held a central position in his own life's outlook. Clearly the casualties of failure felt in divorce for the older man are in reality the products of having lived intensely with a woman and having lived as father with children whose very lives were shaped by his presence among them. The young man's view of himself and his world is to borrow from the philosophers, solipsistic. He is self-centered without being selfish. His self-centeredness is not the result of faulty training in character building but rather the function of a society that spares its young from a too early exposure to the tasks of marriage and family building.

Thus when we speak of the Special Problems of Men after divorce we shall speak of failure not only as each man experiences it, but as our industrialized society unwittingly contributes to his failure. It is important to note here that divorce, *felt* as failure, is *not* failure in fact. Despairing Lionel turned his feeling of failure into a fact of his personal life while Fred viewed his failure as a caution, as an opportunity to correct some hidden problem in his character. One man's failure is another man's opportunity. Were we to take a clinical view of Lionel marrying again without first troubling to correct his special problem, marriage counselors would likely agree that Lionel would be bound to repeat his first marriage or his second marriage, neither one of which, as we shall note later, corrected his special problem as a man. "He who does not learn from experience is bound to repeat it."

The discussion in this chapter largely views the special problem of divorce among men from the broad perspective of how men are socialized in our culture. Man in his family and man at his work must be profoundly understood if we are to illuminate the special problem of men after divorce. Too often the special problem of men after divorce is simplistically and mistakenly met by urging the recently divorced man to virtually lose himself in a round of activity. This view overlooks, and dangerously so, the inner mood of uncertainty and despair which the divorced man may feel, a despair made the deeper because he is everywhere surrounded by optimistic and enthusiastic reports which he knows are false, and indeed which his well-wishers only wish were true.

What we shall be suggesting later in this chapter is that men in our culture are poorly prepared for the loving intimacy of marriage and family and that this neglect often looms formidably above them after they find themselves divorced. This failure at emotional preparation is, as we shall note, more specially the problem of men than of women. And because they fail to grasp this insight even after divorce, their problem is great and their pain difficult to explain.

What follows are two clinical portraits of two men, Lionel and Donald. Our two studies may be seen as widely different characters and indeed they may be regarded as exceptional, if not atypical studies from which to draw generalizations about the special problems of men. Yet within the two studies that follow may be found reliable indications of the special problems of men, all men. For in the lives of Lionel and Donald there has always been a central plaguing doubt which for want of a precise term we may call Commitment—the freedom to make choices. A divorce of a marriage which is not remembered as having been freely chosen is not, as one would think, release from a yoke of bondage. Men are more often distressed over their failure at matters they did not initiate than they suffer over failures in matters they once chose. The Zorba of fiction who looked out at disaster after months of preparation, who saw his efforts crumble at his feet, who laughed at the absurdity of life and proceeded to dance madly amid the rubble, as if by this mad indifference he could defy disaster from possessing him completely, this is the Zorba of illusion and fiction. There are few Zorbas among divorced men. Even Fred who appeared stoical after his divorce found in his divorce the occasion for introspection. The Lionels of this world look out upon their lives as a continuing disaster. Now let us turn to our studies of Lionel and Donald.

Lionel was the only child of immigrant parents. "Ethnics" from southern Europe, his parents settled in central California to live and work with their European countrymen. They were vineyard tenders and fruit growers. They led simple lives. They gathered in the same churches, attended the same festivities, spoke their mother language easily and affectionately. His father was a large affable man who worked in the large gathering sheds where crates were stacked along shaded walls waiting for the huge trucks to load and roll to the market. His mother, alone during the day, worried after Lionel and filled him with fantasies of an adventurous life away from the vineyards, a life lived in the bosom of an imaginary America where glittering success was within reach of the gifted. Lionel grew into a sensitive adolescent twitching nervously at the vague but now overblown fantasies that filled his head. In high school Lionel came upon his first steps toward finding a life away from the towns and villages clustered around the vineyards. Encouraged by his mother he changed his name to Lionel from the softer, though unpronounceable name given at his baptism. At a call for volunteer actors and theater hands at the leading community theater, Lionel discovered the arts. He chose stage design and set painting. He was challenged by the assignment of matching the mood of the play with visual effects he would create. By the time he graduated from high school he had several plays to his credit and his reputation as a creative set designer was well established in his community. Encouraged again by his mother and moved intensely by his own fantasies, he shortly thereafter left the life of his parents and moved to New York where he enrolled for specialized courses in his chosen field of stage and set design.

Two years later in New York he met Marjorie at a little theater company. She was a fashion designer during the day and like Lionel she volunteered her evening hours as wardrobe and costume designer with the theater group. Their work brought them together in their evening hours at the theater, often in their tiny flats where they spent hours matching set to costume, talking colors and lights. Lionel was a worrier, easily frustrated and quickly defeated. When a director tactlessly dismissed a model that Lionel had submitted, only Marjorie would know his suffering. She spoke softly to him, assuring him that his model had more merit than the director could see at first glance. Her gentle encouragement would soon bring Lionel out of his despair and shortly thereafter they were at work again side by side. In time they felt a deepening intimacy between them, though their talk and their behavior never ventured into the intimacy of lovers. Inevitably a time arrived. On a winter's night in Marjorie's flat, the work had gone well and they sat back and talked easily of other things. The wine was warming and both nodded off to sleep sitting beside each other.

Marjorie urged Lionel to sleep the night in her bed. Heavy with sleep, Lionel could only nod assent and fell quickly asleep lying beside Marjorie. She lay awake several moments studying Lionel as he slept, perplexed at the unceremonious ease he displayed in failing to turn to her as a lover. When they awoke in the morning, they drew close and held each other, exploring each other in random movements. Though Lionel felt sexual excitement rise in him, he also felt strangely restrained from carrying his excitement further. Marjorie boldly led his hand to her. He seemed willingly obedient, nothing more.

Thereafter Marjorie and Lionel found sleeping together comfortable and expected. In time their work together attained first success, their partnership in a common craft drew them even closer together. Though their sexual activity never passed beyond the first night they slept together, they were content to satisfy their sexual urgings in random child play. Theirs was a compelling intimacy and on the strength of its comfort and its silent permissiveness to hold each other away from mature adult sexuality, to no one's surprise, they were married. They rented a loft in an industrial building and after weeks of remodeling they turned their loft into an attractive dwelling and workshop. It was the showplace of their social set.

They continued to live as the creative couple in their limited theater world. There were well-paid teaching assignments for both, special theater productions, some television work. They were doing well. Their friends regarded the couple as ideally suited. In a set where casual living together as free thinking lovers was accepted, Marjorie and Lionel's marriage pleased their friends all the more because it seemed carefully planned, intelligently based on deep common interests and on matching personalities.

A year after his marriage Lionel came upon his first adult sexual experience and with it discovered his sexual potency. His mate in this adventure was a bright and attractive student in one of his workshops, recently divorced. It seemed to have happened quite suddenly.

She had casually asked him to join her at her apartment to judge several sketches she had done. Later in bed with the young woman, Lionel felt no restraint in consummating his sexual excitement. He felt joyous, almost grateful. Later that evening, in bed with Marjorie he clung closely to her as if in this embrace of Marjorie he might better understand what had happened hours earlier. He felt no sexual response in his closeness to Marjorie, only a warm reassuring comfort that he had succeeded at something, something he could not boast of to Marjorie. Yet he deeply felt that if Marjorie knew she would be as proud of him as he felt earlier in bed with the young woman.

In the days that followed Lionel seemed suddenly free. There were other sexual encounters, all of them successful, and followed always by clinging close to Marjorie as he lay beside her in their bed finding silent approval in her responding softness. Lionel and Marjorie lay beside each other in their marriage bed ten years and at the end of that decade they were virginal with each other. It was not long before reports and rumors of Lionel's sexual adventures became too widely known to ignore, and Lionel and Marjorie quietly agreed to divorce.

Divorce from Marjorie seemed to endow Lionel with a quiet dignity. He continued in his life's work seemingly free of any signs of emotional collapse which his friends fearfully suspected. His work schedule remained the same. By agreement with Marjorie he remained in the studio-loft while Marjorie took an apartment on the upper west side of Manhattan. When friends spoke to Lionel of his divorce he responded quietly and seemed to be in some other-worldliness. He spoke of the unpredictability of life. He appeared removed in some philosophic mood that lent a suspicious tranquility to his character. But when one spoke of Marjorie and their life together he lauded her with a special touch of dignity in his voice. No, there was no resentment against Marjorie. Yes, he felt a sense of loss he could declare. What he perhaps could not know consciously was that Marjorie's leaving left him with a brief, transient sense of separation that a child might feel after moving from an old neighborhood into another. But they would be friends for life, he vowed.

Three years later he met Ellen. Younger by eighteen years, she was glamorous and uncommonly attractive. She was given to sudden enthusiasms and moved through Lionel's world of theater people, flitting like a restless hummingbird, now here, now there. She seemed to be everywhere and she seemed unattainable. Her restlessness seemed unbounded and for all of these things, and perhaps more, Lionel felt drawn to her. In her he experienced a return of early fantasies of taming the unconquerable, claiming her as his hard-won prize, and then under his spell, he would drain her of her boundless restlessness. He courted Ellen, pacing her madcap ways no matter where her sudden inspirations led them. They sat on the bank of the Hudson River far on the upper west side and threw pebbles in the river at midnight. They drove hours on end over parkways to lunch at a rural bistro in the Berkshires. Yet even as he joined her in these adolescent frolics he maintained a solemn tone in his endless warnings that she must quiet down and take her life and her future more seriously than she seemed to exhibit in her antics. When she would weary of his brief sermons on the value of settling down, she would stand before him and lock her arms around his neck and then rubbing noses affectionately, she whispered, "Lionel, my lion, don't fence me in. . ."

And then once on a madcap week-end filled with unplanned frivolities, they married. Two weeks later Lionel entertained once more in his studio-loft, this time as Lionel and Ellen. But marriage did not contain Ellen. He rarely smiled at her antics. Her only response to his scoldings was her decision to stay away afternoons and evenings. She arrived to the studio-loft either very late in the evening, or on occasion she would not return until the next day at mid-morning. Lionel stormed, demanding her to act responsibly, to take her marriage seriously, but Ellen took to less and less effort at responding to Lionel's scoldings. She continued her own independent way.

One night she did not return. The next morning Lionel found her brief note. She had gone off with Steve, a young actor. They had left the city and would remain away indefinitely. Lionel was free to call a lawyer, if he wanted to. This was farewell. It was then that Lionel fell into a deeply troubling depression. His loneliness was fierce. He spoke of nothing else but Ellen's treachery and his own endless anguishing torments at himself for not offering Ellen more understanding, for not joining her more freely. He blamed himself for driving her out of their marriage. He turned to Marjorie who heard his tormenting complaints silently; occasionally she reminded Lionel of Ellen's youthfulness, but he appeared unaffected by hearing this. His thoughts and his talks with friends kept Ellen predominant, playing one single theme, he had been harsh with her.

Friends encouraged him to date other women. Several friends arranged dinner meetings for Lionel, but none of those he met satisfied him. They were too old, too settled, too obviously intent on marrying. They lacked imagination. Lionel, past forty, balding and sagging at the belly, looked out at his world with the eyes of the young Lionel newly arrived from the vineyards of central California. He remained mindless of his age. He seemed fixated on youthful Ellens, madcaps, adolescent women. And when he would find a young woman who resembled Ellen in manner and in enthusiasms, he would be temporarily lifted. He went about singing her praises, how different she was from the others. And with predictable regularity each would take her leave of him after the first wave of impulses had spent itself.

We now turn to Donald, the second of our two male studies. Donald was an only child. He remembered his childhood pleasantly, until his father turned to habitual gambling. In time his father became a compulsive gambler, often risking his weekly wages, sometimes pawning family jewelry. When Donald was barely eight years of age his mother in company with Donald, fled her husband, explaining her behavior in a note that told of her unhappiness in her life with him. Several days later Donald remembered his father calling for his wife and son to return to him under pledge that he was completely reformed. The little family then started on a new life. They left the city and moved across the continent to California. Donald's father made good on his pledge. In California his gambling ceased and in time he became a man of unusual mildness. He spoke little, smiled little and appeared to go through his days at work and home cocooned behind a shell that kept him withdrawn from close contact with both his wife and his son. However strange this behavior may have appeared to his wife, it was a far more preferred version of her husband than the troublesome gambler of former years.

Donald's mother ruled over the household and took over the role of guide and inspirer to her son. A firm woman of unequivocal views, she spoke to her son of his future with the plain certainty of an army captain outlining a military campaign. He would be a successful man, this was guaranteed to Donald in official tones. He would of course work hard, he would study hard and he would find his reward for these habits as certainly as the sun rises in the morning. The adolescent listened to his mother quietly and appeared to be in full agreement with her plans and predictions. Away from her, however, at school, he was a truant from his classes, and he frequently moved from one mischief to another. When the school authorities discovered him at his pranks and confronted his parents with his mischief, there was the customary shocked scoldings and the expected penitent apologies. Donald barely managed to finish high school.

Following his service with the army he faced what he has since described as a crisis he dared not feel. He was without plans or hopes. He felt impelled by a mounting anxiety to move in some definite direction, to make good on his mother's wishes for him. At a bar one afternoon a friend encouraged him to study accounting. The arguments seemed persuasive, it was an entrance into the world of business, it was a valued professional skill, and though that afternoon Donald scarcely knew the difference between an accountant and a mathematician, he leaped at the suggestion and quickly enrolled in accounting courses at a local college. He pursued his studies with compulsive energy. He studied without interest and often without comprehending. His attention wandered in his classes, his grades were poor, but he felt pressed to continue as if he were being driven by forces out of his control.

He dated easily in this period, and successfully, since Donald reckoned an "easy score" a successful date. Though several of his dates were bright and attractive, he failed to perceive them as whole persons. His dates were experiences that left him with little personal meaning. His women friends were objects that he used but with whom he could not share interior feelings. He acted in all respects like an "as if" character, one who moves through life without being in life. He spoke correctly and smiled appropriately. He conducted himself properly and performed in all customary ways, though he was entirely unaware, it seemed, that there might be more to give, or that more might be expected.

One day he met Phyllis, a plain girl of good and solid family. Phyllis taught school in the elementary grades and took her work seriously. She spoke glowingly of her feelings about her fourth-graders and hearing her Donald felt a secret envy at her absorption in her work. It was something he lacked, he knew. After several months with Phyllis he proposed marriage, largely as he explained to his friends, "because she knows what she wants, that girl."

After twelve years of marriage, long after Donald had completed his professional training and was securely launched as an accountant, and after three children, and nearing the middle of his fortieth year of his life, he fell into despair. His work, his wife, his day to day routine began to pall until it became painfully difficult to rouse himself to a new day. Neither his work nor his wife offered him relief. On the contrary, the sight of his wife and the feel of his office deepened his despair.

It remained for the long hours of counseling in his search for help that his story unfolded. It was a story which when pieced together told of a life following under orders issued by others, his mother, his friends, his wife. He had followed others obediently and not until he had reached his fortieth year that he found himself in a situation that felt alien to him. He asked aloud if others, his wife, his work, owed him something in return for his obedience, some sense of satisfaction of goals achieved, a marriage and family established. When, where were the joys of goals achieved to come to him? Everything he had and had done now seemed dry to the taste.

He took to leaving Phyllis and the children for days, and then would return, only to leave again. Perhaps these absences would help give him a fresh perspective on things, but he used the absences as he used his time in high school. He played the truant in his adult version of an earlier self. There were other women, transient, meaningless encounters, and then another return to Phyllis and the children. In time Phyllis, grieving futilely at his deepening despair, hearing perhaps once too often his frank truth that he felt nothing for her, encouraged him to separate and perhaps divorce. They were divorced within months following one such occasion when Donald reiterated his failure to feel any affection for her.

After his divorce Donald faced the most perplexing of all questions, a question which perhaps had to wait until after his divorce. *What did he really want out of his life?* He took to exhibiting anger at his work and sometimes treated his clients curtly with ill-concealed contempt. His frequent but necessary phone and in-person conversations with his wife left him in a confused state of regret and annoyance. He found it difficult to reflect over the insight that perhaps his work and his wife were not made experiences of his choosing. It was even more difficult to explain to himself what it was that woke him to this impasse in his life. Depressing as these enigmas were, he evinced even more distress at the final question he asked again and again. Was he capable of making choices, could he involve himself in experiences that could capture his will, could he, in short, direct himself to a destiny of his choice?

We return now to the question of how Lionel and Donald, two seemingly disparate personalities, perhaps atypical for our purposes, can illustrate the special problems of men after divorce. Were we to lay out major problem areas gathered from our two clinical portraits along one continuous spectrum we might find significant clues to follow in our search to understand something of the special problems of men who enter the life of the divorced. One central problem that seemed to emerge following the end of Lionel and Donald's marriage was the uncertainty of next steps.

Clearly the man whose reasons for divorce existed in an extramarital relationship, "the other woman" who managed to end the marriage, will not be plagued by the uncertainty of next steps. He brings no special problem in his divorce for he appears to have stepped out of one marriage and into another, virtually by-passing the impact of divorce. But the Lionels and Donalds are not candidates for such certainties in life. Uncertainty has been an unseen but constant companion in their lives.

As Marjorie could not hold Lionel, neither could Phyllis hold Donald. Both men slipped away from their marriages. Both had married idealizations patterned by others. Neither had married personally-felt choices. Both moved through their lives as self-perceived children who depended on others for guidance. In his divorce from Marjorie, Lionel abandoned his idealization, but failed to replace it with another view of himself and his place in the world. Instead he fell back upon early but highly transient feelings that held the lure of excitement, of childhood dreams about to come true. Lionel was drawn to Ellen and to all the later Ellens he met because they promised intense excitement, followed unhappily by the pains of frustration and exploded fantasies. It was only after his divorce from Ellen that Lionel came to sense, and yet feel compelled to enact his special problem again and again in playing the doomed moth to the flame that could only destroy him. For Lionel no problem following his loss of Ellen seemed more acute than his addiction to the alternating intensities of excitement and pain.

For Donald life as a divorced man offered him the same special problems he had known as a man all of his life. He could likewise no longer trust early idealizations, but perhaps even more despairing was his gnawing fear that neither could he trust himself to evolve a self-made view of himself with its hoped for ability to know what was "right" for him.

Parenthetically, it seems clear that the task of the counselor in treating the special problem of divorce with his male client must include a deeper knowledge of his client's total life, sufficient at least to arrive at an understanding of the sources of his client's ideas and idealizations. Side by side with this ongoing effort at understanding the major influences in his early life, the counselor is advised to involve his client actively in this critical review of his past in order that the client may himself grow to understand that ideas and values once accepted by him as guidelines to life may have failed to bring him the satisfactions he had expected. It is at such junctures that the client should be helped to understand the life-long need to so understand one's self that when choices are made, they are felt as extensions of our very selves. Choices then cease to be automatic behavior performed in unconscious obedience to earlier idealizations. In a word, the special problem of men after divorce is the task of mental house-cleaning. As in the Chinese symbols for Crisis, divorce flashes danger to the man who is compelled to repeat his mistake, the man who darkly senses that he is without choice.

The man who chooses to view his divorce as opportunity earns a long overdue breathing space between two time periods in his life. He will use the time for mental house-cleaning and for serious examination of goals to pursue. He thus permits himself to move into new experiences without crippling preconceptions and without ulterior motives. And he will in turn permit himself the freedom to reveal himself without guile.

The reader who assumes that a critical discussion of the special problems of men in divorce must deal in depth and in detail with the customary areas of loneliness, sexual adventuring, separation from children, bachelor living and the host of stark realities that follow from divorce assumes the skills of meter reading to be a prime requisite for the study of physics. The realities of sudden bachelorhood in its day to day problems in living are not problems in depth, they are transient hardships, painful and frustrating though they may be. Neither a "How to" discussion of where a divorced man may expect to find companionship, nor an extended essay on the success/failure probabilities which he may expect to encounter in his sexual pursuits will bring understanding to the central problem as we perceive it.

The Lionels of this world will find emptiness wherever they turn, largely because they live with a sense of inner emptiness. One does not direct a Lionel to the fertile plains of new social opportunities principally because without his conscious knowledge he is obliged to defeat his advisors. He is, without awareness, bound to disappoint his advisors as he must disappoint himself. "How to" directions to the Lionels are doomed to fail. Lionel's very special problem is most sharply met through leading him to understand his own inner need to find triumph in defeat.

Men may differ in their ways of exploring their new life as divorced men. Some may enter that life vigorously, rushing to crowd appointment books with all manner of activity, while others may hang back passively for a time, fearful of testing the water. But in either case, the aggressive and the passive man are both compelled to pause and look out upon their varied experiences, and each will be compelled to understand his life and his new experiences in far different terms than he had settled for in earlier times. Each will be beset by the endless question, of knowing the "real" from the "unreal." He will inevitably sense that awaiting him is the responsibility to distinguish between a way of life that vainly leads outward to activity piled on activity yielding little of the meaning he will need to guide him from the long overdue search into himself. If he avoids the latter, then the doors to meaningful experiences must remain closed to him.

It must be clear, therefore, that one of the tragic myths perpetuated in our society is the often heard notion that the most effective antidote to the loneliness of bachelorhood is instant activity. Activity and social opportunities can of course be palliative, but such a course exclusively pursued is as productive as gathering water in a sieve. Every man recently divorced must know the feeling at the close of his day that though he conformed to the myth—he dated, he socialized, he was kept busy—the emptiness remained.

One may ask how the special problem of men as stated here is essentially different from the problem of women after divorce. If the essential problem for men after divorce rises from a neglected need to understand one's self, to understand one's past, to understand past idealizations, others' goals and values, then it would appear that we have stated a universal problem, one that transcends in scope and depth the special situation of men. Certainly women know the emptiness of meaningless experiences as men do. Certainly women have been known to choose mates who were likewise the illusory creatures of their early idealizations. How then do we claim this universalist problem as essentially a problem of men after divorce?

We make this claim on two main grounds.

1. In most instances, women after divorce continue to live in the same pattern as they did in their marriage. There are notable differences, of course, and these are of major consequence. The absence of husband and father is quickly felt within the broken rhythm of life in the home; there sometimes follows a cessation of an adult social life with other married couples. However major these differences may be, they exist at another level. The problem of divorce for a woman does not so much touch the deeply inner center that a man senses in his anxious feeling of personal failure. The woman's anxiety derives largely from a fear that she may fail at the task of continuing the pattern of home making and child rearing alone.

The divorced woman is perforce preoccupied with survival problems. Imaginative, courageous women often find the period after divorce a rejuvenating opportunity to reenter the world of the salaried employed. They often learn new skills or brush up on old ones. They enroll for courses at nearby schools. Briefly, many women after divorce, following the first shock waves of separation, turn to a form of self-realization by taking on new roles as student or as worker. Divorce frequently leads to an emancipation of old roles for new roles that in time widen an earlier life made stifling by a failing marriage.

2. The male ego, influenced and shaped by a culture that sharply divides life's goals differently between the sexes, is burdened with a special set of expectations. However he perceives success in the specific terms of his ethnic, socioeconomic class, the illusion of success for the male in our society transcends race and class lines. For many men, an unnamed desolation waits them after they find themselves relatively secure economically; it is then they speak of a sense of loss, or emptiness, or disappointment, as though something promised long ago never entered their lives.

Life stories of men told in counselors' offices, theater dramas, movies, novels, all dwell upon the central theme of the emptiness in the lives of men. Tragedy here strikes with double force. At first it brings a pervasive disappointment that something yet lacks in their lives, something beyond economic security or even the appreciation of friends. And then tragedy accents its presence by hints that the something which men vainly yearn after remains elusive, its very form seems beyond human recognition.

On these two main grounds, and in this terribly special sense of man's fate in our society, divorce becomes a special problem of men. If his marriage was a promise and a pledge which he made to himself, if it was for him a special relationship in which he would demonstrate qualities which have been lauded by untold generations, then divorce falls upon him as a shattering instance of personal failure.

Neither our folk culture found in manners and customs, nor our legal culture represented in laws and court decrees expect the divorced man to remain as head of the family which his marriage created. He is separated from house and home. He is removed from the life-flow rhythm he once lived in as husband and father. He is compelled to live elsewhere and he is spared the familiar preoccupations of keeping house and home together. And because of these extra consequences of divorce, his new and strange role of being without role leaves him confused and emptied. He may not take comfort from thoughts of entering new work, or learning new skills. Obviously, this opportunity does not draw him with the same necessity as it draws the divorced woman.

From still another perspective men carry special problems because they are encouraged from childhood on to suppress their feelings, lest they appear as weak before their peers. We shall elaborate on this perspective briefly. Three spheres of existence become increasingly articulated for all of us as we grow into life. Though each sphere calls for different roles and responses from us, we are obliged to perform in each sphere if we are to live full and vital lives.

There is first our early families, the home of our parents and sibs, followed after marriage into the home we create and the family that grows from the marriage. A second sphere is in our work life, school when we are children on to young adult periods in our lives. to be followed by our employment in offices, factories, or in the host of other settings. There is finally the third sphere, the larger world of friends, of organized groups, church membership, political parties. In brief, this is the world in which we express ourselves through our ideas, our ideologies. This latter world of friends and organized groups, important as that world is to round out our existence, is for our immediate purposes here not of primary significance. We are here principally concerned with a view of man as we observe him in the worlds of home and family, and in the world of work. These are the two worlds in which man lives and functions continuously.

We have said that each of these spheres requires different roles and responses, and each draws upon different levels and intensities of psychological functioning. In our families we experience ourselves and our "loved ones" primarily at an emotional level. Our relationships at home are unstructured, spontaneous and affectional. Here we lift restraints and we live freely with all manner of expression of feeling. If as children we cried and raged in our early families, we continue these basic feelings of anger and frustration in our later families, considerably transformed of course in some acceptable adult version. Home is the cathartic center for all of our feelings.

Away from home, at our work, relationships become structured, roles become defined, and our responses are more carefully drawn than we dare at home. In brief, our work atmosphere, though often casual and warm, is rarely a replication of life at home. And for many people the overlay of behavioral restraint imposed by their work setting is felt as a welcome relief. Counselors and therapists are all familiar with men clients who suffer from "week-end" neurosis, a condition characterized by tension at home and an inability to relax at leisure. These men feel closer to some sense of inner comfort in the protected environment at work.

Men in our culture are sometimes encouraged to idealize the work posture. In this posture the human qualities most valuable for success are antithetical to the qualities most desirable for life at home. The work posture becomes not only an idealized image to pursue, it becomes the norm, the standard by which male behavior is to be judged. In consequence, many men resist the free flowing rhythm of give and take, of the highs and lows in mood which characterize life within the bosom of the family. Many confess to the difficulty of "shifting gears" when they reach home after their day at work. Some have solved the problem of the change-over in mood by asking for a brief time alone away from the children in a "decompression chamber" at home.

Yet in a study of six thousand men, aged 45 to 54, which sought to relate work success with marital success, it was found that those men who progressed furthest in their careers were still married to first wives. Next came the remarried. Divorced, separated and widowed men trailed badly. For perhaps a special group of men who over-idealize the work posture, easy access to emotional expression appears to be shut off. These men describe scenes from their lives at home which find them standing mute and helpless as their wives pour out their rage at the now legendary charge of "no communication." And sadly, perhaps, these men later justify their silence by characterizing their wives' behavior as childish. In time these men grow immune to angry demands for communication.

The idealized image of the successful man hence becomes a liability for many men. Admittedly, not all men in our work society are so addicted to the idealized image of the successful man. The marginally skilled laborer, the chronically unemployed, are likely burdened so early in life with the encompassing problems of poverty that their value systems are closely related to problems far more immediate than illusions of a distant success. Clearly the population we are dealing with are men over 34 years of age, engaged in work pursuits that provide built-in potentials for advancement to positions of greater responsibility and more remuneration.

In the main, we have been observing men who appear to be psychologically split, condemned to live emotional live and mental lives which are not only widely separated one from the other, but in which the mental life style adopted for the work setting threatens to eclipse the emotional life, draining it of passion and feeling. More than women, the man stands awkwardly above these two worlds of home and work. While he is at least accounted a full partner in his home, in governing the affairs of his family, with immediate access to a position of power, at his work setting he is often far removed from the center of power. When he thinks of power and its uses in the hands of the successful man, he envisions qualities and forms of human expression that are calculated to inspire others to emulate such traits. Thus he prizes silence and the visage of thoughtfulness. The outer hint of inner strength and stability is conveyed by a behavior of reserve. At home, however, these qualities could only earn him attack for standing at a distance and for being uncommunicative.

In large part, therefore, the special problem of men after divorce is suggested here in the psychological ability to live comfortably in the two separate worlds of home and work, a phenomenon which our industrialized society has created for all of us. The casualties of this split may be seen in those men who are unable to shift gears as they pass from one sphere to the other. The traditional model of the autonomous family, classically structured in the hierarchy of father, mother, eldest son, daughters, working side by side in the fields in the shadow of home has long since passed. Nevertheless it is that model which stubbornly hovers over us as the idealization of an entire society; it has by now become our folk mythology.

When a man can authentically *feel* his role of husband and father, he will function in these roles without difficulty. To reverse matters, to assume that to function in human roles without feelings appropriate to the role is to live imitatively. It may be a truism to say that divorce as an event in the life of a man bears an analogous significance as the sneeze does to the cold. Both are symptoms of a hidden problem. And though divorce may be a one-event experience in the total flow of life's experiences, it can also be a bottle-neck and seriously impede the free flow of other experiences unless attention is directed to it quickly.

Centuries ago men rose from apparent preoccupations with passions and condemned themselves for their failure to structure their universe. From Plato to Descartes, only the mind of man, its special capacity for reason was celebrated. Spinoza himself, the poet of reason, spent a bland life decrying man's bondage to passion. When this legacy touched our shores our Puritan forebearers enshrined virtue as righteous behavior, and righteous behavior was measured in emotion-free behavior. The special problem of men today is made even more acute by the rapid emancipation of women who no longer follow men's models of behavior. They are no longer passive and submissive before their husband's will. The danger may yet be that women in their understandable struggle for emancipation will read the new role behavior in sexual terms and hence choke off the sources of passion under a synthetic political fiat.

LaRochefoucald once observed, "It is harder to hide feelings we have than to feign those we lack." This may well state the special burden which man has taken on to himself. The men we speak of here may have subordinated their behavior at home and thus emerged as partial persons, a too valuable price to pay for a view which regards behavior at home as trivial and inconsequential. "He who can take no interest in what is small will take false interest in what is great." This, perhaps, is the tragic mistake of modern man, according to John Ruskin.

CHAPTER 5

SPECIAL PROBLEMS OF WOMEN

HELEN ZUSNE

ARE A WOMAN's problems of adjustment to divorce different from a man's? This depends on her age, background, habits, personality, the way in which she has viewed a wife's role in marriage, and her current attitude toward divorce. The ages of children, if any, and the number of children still at home contribute to the complexity of the situation. While many of the problems that a woman faces are like those of her former husband—problems related to loneliness, depression, anger, guilt, and shock—there are in addition certain problems unique to women, or at least occurring much more frequently in women than in men. The counselor needs to recognize that marriage does not have the same significance for men as for women. To a woman marriage is more important. She is more ego-involved in making her marriage work, and it is often her whole reason for existence. Therefore the impact of divorce is much greater on a woman than on a man.

In the following discussion it is not assumed that every woman faced with divorce is confronted with all the possible problems. To the extent that a woman is self-sufficient and independent in outlook and actions, her problems are less distinguishable from those of men. If she is a person with many interests outside her home, interests which she has not necessarily shared with her husband, or if she has been employed, has handled her own business affairs, or has shared in the handling of family finances, she will be in better shape to cope with divorce. But if her entire life since her marriage has revolved around her husband and her children (or only the husband after the children have left); if she has cleaned the house only to please him, prepared only the foods that he liked, never the ones she enjoyed; if her whole purpose in living has centered around him and she has little else in life that interests her, then the jolt of a divorce can be staggering. Her problems will be very different from those of her husband.

INITIAL PROBLEMS

During the time just after the decision to divorce has been made, and while the terms of the divorce settlement are being considered, your client will need a chance to ventilate her feelings, require considerable support, practical suggestions, and even direct advice. This initial period is especially difficult and frustrating for the wife because she is required to make important decisions at a time when she may not be in the proper frame of mind to do so. Her judgment is apt to be poor and her thinking foggy, although this is by no means always the case. The husband is one up on the wife at this time because he probably has had an opportunity to know more about the family's financial situation as well as business in general. The counselor does not need to give legal advice or play the part of a financial advisor, but he may need to call attention to some of the matters which need to be taken care of, but of which the wife is not aware. For instance, the wife needs to know something about the family income and budget and be able to make at least a gross estimate of how much she needs to support herself and any children who may be living with her according to her present standards or to just tolerable standards. It is surprising how many women do not know how much their husbands make a year, what insurance there is, or whether or not there is a savings account, investment program, or retirement plan. She needs help in choosing an attorney who will understand her needs and help her to decide what a fair and reasonable settlement would be.

At this time each woman needs to be protected from the harmful effects of her own particular emotional reaction, no matter what it may be. The counselor needs to be aware that while some women react with bitterness and hate that turns to greed, others try to be noble, play the martyr role and rashly proclaim that they can get along with no property or support money at all. Few women can afford the luxury of telling their husbands, "I don't want anything from you, not one little penny."

Before she is confronted with papers to sign and even before she sees an attorney, the woman needs to talk over with her counselor what her plans are concerning the couple's children. She will want to decide what she would prefer in the way of visitations. Later discord between the couple can be minimized if there are definite arrangements for visits from the parent who does not have custody, so that there will be no doubt or misunderstanding on the part of anyone. It may also save some worry about late support payments if arrangements can be made for the money to go through the court rather than to be paid directly to the wife. Some women who become temporarily unable to cope with their responsibilities toward their children because of the emotional shock they are experiencing, in desperation allow the husband, or grandparents, to take over the custody of the children temporarily, only to regret their decision later when they attempt to regain custody. If the woman is experiencing severe emotional reaction the counselor needs to take the steps necessary to prevent her from behaving in such a way that she may lose her children. Sometimes hospitalization is necessary.

After the divorce has legally taken place, there are aggravating circumstances confronting the new divorcée. It may even seem to her for a time that people are ready to kick her when she is down. For instance, in order to have a telephone in her name in the house where she may have lived for years, she must make a deposit required of new users; or, after having been employed and having paid for her own clothes and car for years, she now discovers that all credit was her husband's, and that she has no credit anywhere in town. She may have little experience with such matters as mortgages, transferring titles, paying utilities, income tax returns, car, health, and accident insurance.

LETTING PEOPLE KNOW

Many women suffer "untold" agonies before they are able to tell their friends, acquaintances, neighbors, family members, and their children's teachers that they have been divorced. This suffering is unnecessary, and the new divorcée needs to gain some understanding of her own attitudes about divorce in order to manage this hurdle. In general, it is best to inform others soon after the decision is firmly made and legal steps have been taken. Not only does this bring a feeling of relief, but children will feel less strain when the situation is handled in a frank, brief, and matter-of-fact way.

Usually it is the husband who packs up and moves out, leaving the wife in the old neighborhood with the task of explaining what has happened to friends and neighbors. The wife may, however, attempt to keep on in her old ways, hoping neighbors will not notice that her husband's car is around very little and at unusual times. She may pretend to herself as well as others that this awful thing is not really happening to her. To this extent she is not facing reality. Her attitude toward divorce may always have been inappropriately negative. Possibly she has been taught by family and church that divorce is "sinful." She may have been critical, in the past, and intolerant of her friends and acquaintances who have divorced and looked down upon them as failures or as being in some way inferior. Now she cannot bear to face the facts because to do so would require her to be critical of herself, and to consider herself a failure. She may therefore use any defense she can muster to keep on as usual, throwing herself into various activities, keeping excessively busy, refusing to be aware of the change. The day comes, of course, when she must be aware of the facts and must handle her resulting depression.

Telling others about it can help her face the facts. If she cannot on her own muster enough courage, she will need the help of a counselor in handling intense feelings of humiliation and disgrace which stem from an unaccepting, intolerant attitude toward divorce and a feeling that she is somehow above such a thing. She may not believe that her friends and neighbors can be understanding until she gives them a chance. They can help her by their attitude to be more accepting of her situation and more tolerant of herself.

In counseling, rehearsal of what to say to neighbors when the opportunity arises may be helpful. It is not necessary to go into long explanations, to blame anyone, or to air one's anger or hate. Better alternatives are: "It has been a difficult winter. Jim and I are getting a divorce," or, "You probably have noticed that Jim hasn't been here much lately. We're getting a divorce."

This is a time when many women need help in keeping their anger from spreading so that it appears directed at friends who have been uninvolved in the divorce. "How's John these days?" Mr. Peabody asks innocently of the recently divorced Melba. She lashes back at him with a sarcastic remark which leaves Mr. Peabody feeling as if John was surely wise to leave this horrible vixen. It is helpful to anticipate such questions and to discuss ways in which a defensive attitude is inappropriate and leads to unnecessary embarrassment, hurt, and perhaps loss of friends.

In the past the stigma of divorce has clung more to the woman than to the man, no matter what the precipitating circumstances. This is changing, at least to some extent. The old taboos against divorce are crumbling. A counselor can be of help here. "Divorcée" need not be a dirty word, and one need not act as if it were.

COPING WITH AN EX-HUSBAND

It is almost impossible for the relationship with a husband to be cut off instantly, cleanly, with complete lack of pain as soon as a divorce takes place. Business matters, division of property, and especially care of children and arrangements for visitations require some communication. Too much involvement with an ex-husband, however, is a risky business and puts both partners under constant strain. There are very few couples who are fortunate enough to go through a divorce and remain true friends, able to give advice and help to each other when needed while maintaining a casual, easy-going relationship. Such an ideal "divorce relationship" is something to hope for but not to expect, especially in the months and perhaps years immediately following a divorce. If one of the former partners must be constantly warding off hostile verbal attacks or feelings of guilt over the reactions of a former mate who cannot adjust to divorce, or if children are used as a means of continuing unsolved conflicts, then the chances for a friendly, casual, and relaxed relationship are indeed dim.

Overinvolvement with a former mate can be initiated by either the man or the woman, or both. Because women often tend to fit themselves into the role of a dependent, subject to the wishes of the head of the household, they have more difficulty than men in remaining independent when a former mate becomes aggressive in his efforts to reestablish contact.

Some couples experience the trauma of divorce repeatedly. Jan and Mark were married, then divorced two years later while students at a large university. Out of sense of guilt Mark kept reappearing to take out his tearful, depressed ex-wife, to be kind to her, to help atone for the hurt he felt he had caused her. Each time her hope was reestablished only to be dashed again. For a while they would get along fairly well, but then the original conflicts loomed again. A period of time would then go by without Mark appearing, so Jan would look him up. They were unable to keep from seeing each other. Finally, not able to stand it any longer and close to a complete nervous breakdown, Jan left for a visit with relatives half a continent away. Soon Mark followed her, only to discover anew that he and his ex-wife could not get along. Now back at the university, he is attempting to apply himself to his studies and a job. But the cycle will repeat itself for Jan also is planning to return.

Counselors can remind the client that she decided once that she could not make a go of it with her husband and that her decision was thoroughly considered. She needs to be encouraged to stick by her decision and to know that it is possible to get over loneliness and depression. If she gives herself a chance for readjustment and recovery she will eventually want to make new friends. To change her mind constantly or to allow him to change it and to keep plunging herself into painful situations over and over again can destroy her emotionally. By the time she takes legal action, or at least by the time the divorce is finalized, the woman needs to have worked through her ambivalence and will know how to handle her tendencies to change her mind about divorce, or to swing back between love and hate.

Not only is it important for her to recognize and protect herself from her own tendency to vacillate about what she really feels about the man she has divorced, but it is also necessary to understand in what way her ex-husband's feelings affect his behavior. With such an understanding she can keep from being sucked into a situation where conflicts and inner turmoil become so intense that the predivorce problems seem mild in comparison.

A newly divorced woman often needs assistance in coping with an ex-husband who comes around presenting problems. Ex-husbands come in various common varieties.

1. There is the ex-husband who refuses to consider himself divorced, at least where his wife is concerned. He may use as justification the idea that he is morally and spiritually married even though he is legally divorced. It seems to make little difference to him who initiated the divorce proceedings. Such a man may drop in uninvited at any time of day or night, embarrassing his ex-wife in front of guests, for instance. He may phone frequently with a minor excuse, or none at all. He may consider what was once joint property as still belonging to him. He may even pick up and take with him a piece of property which was awarded his ex-wife in the settlement. He may ignore plans made concerning the children and he may give them directions contrary to those given them by their mother while they are in her custody, and even promise them outings which he knows their mother cannot approve of. He may descend like Santa Claus bringing expensive groceries his ex-wife cannot afford and expect to be invited to eat with the family at any time.

This kind of man may feel that he is still in authority and may give instructions or ultimatums to his ex-wife about how she should handle her personal affairs and conduct her business. Many a divorced woman is plagued by being constantly watched or followed as the ex-husband attempts to keep up with her comings and goings, especially if he hears that she is dating. He may even react with the righteous indignation of the married man whose wife is stepping out with another man. It is not at all unheard of for a former husband to expect to be treated with affection and to feel hurt when his ex-wife bristles and stiffens after his attempt to embrace or to kiss her. To react to such a man with anything but distance and coldness is to invite behavior on his part that makes him increasingly difficult to handle.

It appears that such a man wants all the advantages of being married as well as those of being single. He may use his knowledge of his former mate's dependency to wrangle his way back into the marriage, even though that may not really be what he wants. He may come to fix a leaky faucet, to repair the TV antenna, mow the lawn, even babysit. His former mate needs help to keep from returning to her old situation, unable to be free to let the old wounds heal or to start a new life.

Some men who accept divorce initially and allow their wives to adjust in peace for perhaps years, may suddenly come apart at the seams when they discover that their old discarded property has become valuable to another man. It is like an old coat—they don't want it until someone else appreciates it because of its warmth, wearing qualities, or good workmanship. If these men descend on their ex-wives who plan to remarry, they can cause a great amount of trouble at a crucial time when their former mates are trying to help the children to adjust to a stepfather.

A self-sufficient, immovable front, firmness, almost coldness are necessary in order to cope with the man who cannot accept the reality of the divorce. His ex-wife often needs support to keep from showing compassion, for if she does he may try even harder to become involved again.

2. Then there is the ex-husband who has a need to complete unfinished business, who is compelled to continue arguments, to attempt to settle issues, win verbal battles, or to perpetuate with his ex-wife the disturbed relationship which led to the divorce in the first place. Of course, it can be the wife who haunts her ex-mate in an effort to work through old grievances or to continue the disturbed relationship. She needs to recognize her urge to have it out "once and for all" with her ex-partner. With the help of a counselor she may be able to discipline herself and to avoid the temptation to start it all over again.

She needs to be aware when this is what *he* wants to do in order to keep from being drawn into a conversation about details of past misunderstandings. The counselor may go over with her the ways in which to avoid all unnecessary contacts, and at the same time be courteous, businesslike and brief when encounters are necessary. The counselor will assist the client by letting her rehash these subjects in counseling sessions rather than with her ex-spouse. Some of the common rehash subjects which women are tempted to discuss with their ex-spouses are:

"If you had ever let me make one decision on my own. . ."

"If you had only taken me out to a movie, or dinner, or something at least once a month. . ."

"Nothing I ever did satisfied you. If you had ever given me one compliment. . ."

"You always cut me down. . ."

"You never appreciated how I worked for you and the children. . ."

"If you hadn't always sided with your mother. . ."

"If you'd just had the common courtesy to call when you were going to be late for dinner. . ."

"You never really did love me, did you?"

"Let me ask you just one question: why did you do what you did?"

"All you ever thought about was yourself. You never cared what I wanted."

If the goal is adjustment to divorce, she must let the old cat die. One last nasty phone call, one more meeting to hash it all out, one more letter will keep old wounds from healing and will keep the client absorbed in past troubles to the extent that she cannot look forward to a new future.

3. There is still another kind of ex-husband many women must cope with. He is the one whose feelings of guilt are so intense that he must continually work at assigning blame for failure of the marriage to his ex-wife. His guilt may be directed toward either the events that occurred during the marriage or to the divorce itself. It seems to make little difference who first wanted the divorce. Such a man may be unable to keep from contacting his ex-wife in some way in order to throw the load of guilt in her lap.

The ex-wife needs to be wise to the game of tossing the blame load back and forth, so that she can stand her ground against maneuvers directed toward enticing her to play. Even though her first impulse may be to defend herself against unfair accusations and distorted "facts," she must realize that to do so will only make him try harder to blame her. Her ex-mate may need help in handling crippling guilt feelings, but all she can do is to assure him that she does not blame him, that both are responsible, and bring the conversation quickly to a close.

If your client understands some of the reasons for her ex-spouse's behavior she can save herself painful reactions to his tricks. It is as if his illogical feelings direct him to make her feel as miserable as he does by making her feel guilty so that he will feel less miserable. There are numerous ways in which a man can work at making his former wife feel guilty. He may preach and moralize using religious doctrines and Biblical quotations to back him up. He may put on the pathetic Peter act presenting himself as sad, alone, depressed, with no one to fix his meals or wash his clothes, and with no money left in the bank—the innocent, hurt one. Of course, his depression can very well be genuine, but if he goes out of his way to point out the tear drops on his letters to make sure his ex-wife knows he is suffering, there is probably a need on his part to make her feel guilty. Some divorced men continue this kind of behavior for the benefit of their ex-spouses even after remarrying and making an excellent recovery from divorce by any standard. The woman who has never seen her husband in tears, apologetic, humble, making declaration of intentions to change may be taken in by such behavior in her ex-husband and may actually feel that she is somehow completely responsible for his misery.

The unconscious need to project blame upon his ex-wife may push a man to treat her with unusual attention and apparent kindness which may mask for a while his feelings of hostility. It is difficult for her to react to kindness by being cold and ungrateful without also feeling guilty. It is not uncommon to hear declarations of intense love coupled with hostile critical remarks. So we have a man who not once remembered an anniversary while he was married sending flowers to his ex-wife on the anniversary of their marriage with a note: "You are a wonderful woman, and I would give the world to be married to you. I have never known anyone who could be so cold, deceitful, and mean."

Of all the difficult relationships with an ex-husband none are so painful as those pertaining to their children. Difficulties may revolve around misunderstanding or selfishness regarding arrangements for visitations, or conflicts over discipline, or whatever else the mother sees in the behavior of her ex-husband which she considers harmful to the children or as taking advantage of her. Often to defend herself makes the situation more difficult for her children. The husband may promise to come take the child on an outing and then never show up, and it is the mother who must comfort the waiting, disappointed child. He may shower the child with gifts, attentions, and excursions at one time, then neglect him for long periods; or perhaps he may give the child a longed-for bicycle which the child is then not allowed to take home. The father may subtly or openly berate his ex-wife in front of the children. He may use the children as a means of invading his ex-wife's privacy as he milks the children about what is going on at home. The divorcée who finds herself getting extremely angry over her husband's handling of the children needs a chance to ventilate her anger in counseling sessions, and then to plan on a reasonable course of action which will not cause the situation to escalate.

Adjustment to divorce is never completely over. The years spent with one man leave their permanent effects, both good and bad. One morning Marge was sipping coffee at the breakfast table, across from John, her second husband, to whom she had been married seven years. She suddenly remembered something she wanted to tell him, and out of the blue came "Roger. . ." She stopped short, clapping her hand over her mouth, realizing too late that she had called her first husband's name. The awkward silence, after a sheepish glance, was relieved with a "Pow" from John across the table. The old lament of the divorced, "all those wasted years," is not really so. The past is over, and what happens in the present or in the future cannot change it—or make good experiences of the past into bad experiences.

When the shock, the loneliness, and the bitterness and ambivalence have faded away, what can be considered the ideal attitude for a divorcée to have toward her former mate?

1. Understand his behavior for what it really is in an unbiased unemotional way.

2. Caring for him as an individual with his own problems, feelings, and right for happiness, an individual for whom she has concern and good wishes, but with whom she does not wish to be closely involved.

3. Refusing to repeat endlessly old conflicts, or to be put in an intolerable situation by him.

4. Firmly insisting that living go on in the present, with an optimistic outlook toward a future which does not include marriage to an ex-husband.

5. Allowing memories of her past marriage to present themselves without dwelling on them or being caught up in intense emotions.

6. Regaining perspective and a sense of humor.

COPING WITH CHANGE

Drastic changes in life style often accompany a divorce. With women more often than with men these changes occur in almost every area of life and reach staggering proportions. Even to the woman with personality traits of exceptional flexibility and resilience, such widespread changes coming simultaneously can be shocking, and can bring on fatigue, depression, and anxiety.

It is not just the empty chair by the television set or the absence of men's shirts in the laundry. Nor is it even the quietness which comes with the absence of bickering, arguments, and accusations. A divorced man also has such adjustments to make. A whole new way of life often emerges. Thus we see a woman who has never held a job in her life attempting to earn a living, or a woman in her forties or fifties who has never pushed a lawn mower or done yard work exerting herself with sweat on her brow. Unless she is one of the few whose husbands were financially well off and she was able to get a generous divorce settlement, she will need to change her standard of living. Menu planning, meal preparation, shopping habits may have to change radically. She may even have to buy clothes at different shops that carry cheaper brands. If she has children, she finds that, in addition to other changes, she has less time to spend with them. To hold down a job she must leave her children with a sitter or at a nursery. If her children are too old for that, she may have to leave them alone after school hours and worry about whether they are able to handle their new freedom wisely.

Perhaps after a day at an unaccustomed job she comes home with swollen feet and aching back to find that her children have been uncooperative and have failed to do their assigned tasks. She may react with unusual irritability, only to experience endless repercussions as children react to mother's new demands and to her fatigue and irritability. It is no wonder that a percentage of women completely give up at this point. They are usually the ones with no experience or preparation for making a living, with a number of small children and very little support money, or with little confidence in themselves as individuals. Some of these women are forced back into an intolerable marriage or must give up custody of their children because they do not know how to handle the flood of new responsibilities with the resources available. Some of these tragedies could be avoided if the women would seek counseling and guidance at a community social agency or with a private psychologist or counselor, where they could learn to handle practical problems better and receive the necessary emotional support.

The initial shock of widespread change subsides as time passes. The picture is not all black for there are many positive results which accompany the upheavals. In spite of the probable shortage of money, time, and energy and the burden of responsibilities never before assumed, many women find their new life stimulating, challenging, even invigorating. The imprisoned housewife who has known only diapers and dishes now is forced to become involved with other people at her new job, and she feels more a part of the world outside the house. The pampered housewife who has been preoccupied with her own care may be forced to become a more useful and thus a more interesting person to herself as well as to others. The rigid, self-righteous woman who has been roughly jolted from her smug and proper rut now is in a position to be more accepting and understanding of other people's problems, thus stretching her capacity for empathy with others.

When a newly divorced woman joins the ranks of the employed after a decade or more of unemployment, she experiences first hand the problems common to most employed women. Inequities and discrimination against women in the job market can be tolerated more easily by a woman whose marriage is stable and whose husband has an income which is more than adequate. Such a woman may be working for her own enjoyment or for frills, such as a summer vacation or a new swimming pool. Even the woman who has only herself to provide for has an easier time and is less bothered by inequities than the breadwinner of a family of seven people. Consider the new divorcée, as she is still smarting from unfair treatment she feels she received at the hands of one man, who tries to provide adequately for herself and her family. Even the most intelligent, ambitious, and capable of women may be in for a disillusioning experience that may leave her sour not only toward her ex-husband but toward men in general, and even toward a society that allows such prejudices and unfair practices toward working women to exist.

During early years of marriage when a woman is busy with domestic duties and is contented, even flattered, to be cared for by a man on whom she can lean, she may not be confronted with the problems of women's rights in the working world. The problem does not touch her then for she is enjoying her role and fitting in with the old traditional viewpoint of a woman's place being in the home. But after divorce, along with all the other changes, there is a new orientation toward herself and society, and she discovers that her ideas about women's place in the world have also changed.

George and Mary started dating steadily when they were both in the eleventh grade. George was an average student and he applied himself inconsistently to his studies. When he and Mary studied together his grades improved somewhat. She enjoyed school, was a brilliant student in a class of over four hundred. They were both eager to get married, but managed to wait until they were half-way through their sophomore year at the state university. Both sets of parents were opposed to the marriage, but George and Mary felt they could manage on their own, and they did. Mary dropped out of school and took a job at the University's Bursar's office where she worked full time until her husband had his Master's degree. The only interruption was a few months when their first child was born. They then moved to another city, and George was pleased with his first job and his income which was much more, of course, than Mary's had been. He worked hard, and during the years received several promotions. Meanwhile Mary enjoyed the luxury of being at home with her babies. As her children grew older and George was more than ever absorbed with his job, the responsibility for the children fell completely to her. She was active in Scouts and PTA and worked hard as a mother and housewife—but received no salary. George's work kept him out later and later as he found it necessary to meet his clients for dinner and drinks and to socialize in order to increase his sales. The marriage deteriorated as his drinking and her nagging increased and their positive involvement with each other faded away. The divorce settlement granted Mary a fine home, only partly paid for, and $100 monthly for support of each of three children who were not yet eighteen. At age 43, after not having worked for almost twenty years, Mary looked for a job. Although she was neat and young in appearance, she was turned down a number of times because she was too old or because she had not been working recently. Finally she found a job at $400 a month. She worked as a secretary to a young executive who came to depend on her for major decisions and much of the actual work involved in his job. With the child support, Mary had an income of $700 a month for herself and her three children (or four —until her 19-year-old daughter could support herself). Her ex-husband, on the other hand, had a balance of $1500 each month (after paying child support) with which to support himself and his new wife.

Mary was actually lucky when compared to the majority of divorced women who seek jobs after a long period of unemployment. She at least had some valuable, although not recent, work experience. She was neat-appearing, intelligent, and had some positive regard for herself as an individual. She could manage financially on what she received, but even with all this going for her she could not help but be acutely aware of the inequities which penalize working women at every turn. Her husband George was no more deserving, had worked no harder in his life, had even less potential than she when both were juniors in high school. Even if she had continued her education along with her husband, the chances are indeed slight that she could have been able to match him with respect to job responsibilities or salary. Thus one important change that many divorcées experience is a turnabout in attitude toward a woman's role in marriage and in the world of work.

No matter what the women's liberation movement may mean to an individual, or how ridiculous some of their extreme ideas may sound, at least it has made the general public aware of the unfair practices toward women which exist in employment. Improvements have been made, but there is still a long way to go before a qualified woman can be on equal grounds with a man in most job situations. Until then the new divorcée must cope with the situation which exists, hoping to find an area where discrimination is at a minimum and remembering that there are men who share her viewpoint. She must console herself by telling herself that the amount of income does not measure happiness, feelings of self-worth, or individual freedom.

The divorced woman whose children are grown has problems which are somewhat different. If she is employed, the change in her life which may bother her most is dealing with the quietness of a house when she comes home from work. Many women who come for counseling after a divorce report that they can cope well in the daytime, but are tormented by the empty house in the evening. They try a poodle with a noisy collar, an unwatched TV turned to a high volume, or moving out of the house to an apartment complex where walls are thin and noises abound. The mature woman who has never been employed and who has already suffered depression and a feeling of uselessness since her children have left home for college or homes of their own, now has problems which are actually agonizing. Her children no longer need her, and neither does the man to whom she was married for perhaps most of her life. Such an individual must start from scratch to find new, useful activities, new friends, and people to help, all of which can keep her from turning her attention inward, toward herself. With professional help she may discover a new purpose in life.

A young woman without children should have an easier time handling changes brought about by divorce, because her patterns of behavior are not as deeply ingrained. It should be easier for her to consider her marriage that has just ended a valuable experience which has helped her learn more about herself and the nature of intimate relationships. She may even wish to change back to her maiden name. It is not necessary to use the title "Mrs." and advertise to everyone who notices the absence of a husband that she has once been married.

Some women can tolerate more change than others. They may decide that while they are changing from the married to the unmarried state they will also make a number of other major changes which are not compulsory. It is not unheard of for a woman to get away completely from the old setting—a new town, new state, new job—and make a fresh start. Whether to undertake such a radical change depends on some practical considerations. Are there friends and relatives nearby? Can the new divorcée tolerate loneliness until she can make friends? Is the move economically feasible? Will there be a tendency to cling in an unhealthy way to grown children in the vicinity? Is the move motivated merely by a desire to escape the imagined or real reactions of friends and relatives of the divorcée? If the change is a running back to a childhood home with mother and dad, it will probably not be one which will facilitate a healthy adjustment to divorce.

Excessive change is a shock and strain even when conditions improve with change. Changes that accompany divorce are usually more extensive and complex for women than for men. It is a wise women who seeks professional help during this difficult period.

RELATIONSHIP WITH MEN

A satisfactory adjustment to divorce has not been achieved until your client is free to establish mutually satisfying relationships with men, whether these are intimate, long-term relationships or casual everyday encounters. Let us consider some of the difficulties in relating to men which often occur as reactions to or as extension of difficulties with the man just divorced. The following ways of reacting are some with which the marriage counselor will become familiar.

1. Bitterness. Mabel Fry treats all men in an impersonal, cold, and distant way. Any man who has occasion to have conversation with her feels her unspoken hostility, and transacts his business quickly to make an exit. She perceives all men as selfish animals who have designs on her as a possible handy receptacle for their semen.

2. Live it up. Lucille Fling overreacts to her freedom. Although for years she has been ultra proper, she now embraces poorly considered experiences with any man available. She feels she has missed something and now she is hunting desperately for it in the most unlikely places.

3. Fear of rejection. Molly Small longs for and needs a relationship with a man, but she is unable to allow herself to be really close to anyone for fear she will be hurt again.

4. Ten down and hundreds to go. What better way can Sandie Bell express her hatred for men than by loving and leaving them. The more notches in her chastity belt the better. Although she believes that she loves all men, it gives her an unconscious delight to be seductive, make them fall for her, and then hurt them as she has been hurt.

5. So sweet to compete. Harriet Smart felt inferior to and belittled by the man she was once married to. Now she attempts to zoom ahead as an aggressive, industrious, efficient, and ambitious woman, rebelling, proving her worth, competing fiercely. While her reaction may result in worthwhile accomplishments, it will not help her to establish a stable relationship with men.

6. Propping up a sagging ego. Her husband never seemed to care,

so little wonder that Janice Redman felt like a real woman when she found out that there existed a man who enjoyed making love to her. So she tried it again with another man, and again, and again. . . Oddly enough, no matter how often she propped up her ego, when morning came it had sagged again. She could never form a real relationship, because she was concentrating on quantity rather than quality in her relationships with man.

7. Daddy, help poor little me. Darlene Clingon has an air of innocence about her that the boys fall for, and she uses it to get job promotions, attention, and extra favors from neighbors, who mow her lawn and help her fix her car. She gives them a sweet smile and lowers her curly lashes over her big brown eyes. And that's it! She has never had the capacity for a mature relationship with a man, but she enjoys the admiration and attention which her dependent manner evokes.

The divorcée's relationship with men is complicated by the way men regard a divorcée. Many men think that the divorced woman is a sex-starved hot mamma ready to jump into bed with any man who crooks his little finger. The divorced woman who finds a job as a secretary often has more than her share of problems in handling the boss who feels he has the right to handle her wherever and whenever he chooses. A number of recently divorced women are forced to give up badly needed jobs because they do not know how to resist advances on the part of their bosses without offending them. They may need help to learn how to respond in any easy, light manner, using some flattery to build up the boss's ego while giving a firm "no" which may get the message across to him without causing him to be angry.

Many men do not understand the nature of a woman's sexual needs, which they feel are as immediately pressing and urgent as their own. Your client may not understand how to cope with such men without increasing her bitterness and resentment which prevent her from having a reasonable relationship with any male. Clients report incidents in which the husband of a best friend, or a neighbor they have known and trusted for years calls around to offer his help in satisfying the sexual needs of the recently divorced woman. If she reacts to what the man feels is a generous offer by becoming angry, he may feel that she really has a problem and is indeed a prude. It is a common complaint that if a divorcée accepts a date, her escort assumes that she will want to go to bed with him, as, of course, some women do. At this point many divorcées become soured on all men and decide to eke out a lonely existence without them.

Denial of sexual need is not the best solution for the divorced woman. How she handles her needs depends on many factors: how capable she is of attracting men; what are her neurotic reactions to men; what are her moral and religious convictions; what are her underlying attitudes toward sex and to what extent can she accept her own sexual needs; how rigid is her personality structure; and what her ability to compromise is in the handling of conflicts.

Sublimation, or the draining off of sexual energy by engaging wholeheartedly in a constructive activity, is a workable emergency measure for a few women who are athletically talented or are creative individuals who paint, compose, or write. The day arrives, however, when sublimation is not enough.

Mechanical means can be used by some women to relieve specific and recognized tensions which are sexual in nature. Many women, however, are shocked, offended, and repulsed by the idea of masturbation. In counseling with such women the subject must be approached in an indirect, descriptive way rather than offered as an idea that the divorcée can use. Attitudes change slowly, and advice given to a woman before she can accept it will be useless. Masturbation is a substitute measure, at best, which fails to offer the warmth, understanding, and feeling of belonging that must accompany the sex act to make it a satisfying experience to most women.

Sex with just any male is not the right solution for the majority of women. What many men fail to understand is that for most women the act of sex itself is not satisfying, regardless of the occurrence of an orgasm, unless the woman feels that there exists between the two people a genuine emotional involvement with a feeling of commitment, some degree of permanence in the relationship, mutual respect, and empathy for each other.

The woman with rigid ideas of right and wrong finds that her need for intimate involvement with men clashes with her need to follow a strict, unbending code of ethics. It takes time and patience on the part of both client and counselor for such a woman to gain insight and to become understanding and accepting of her own conflicting needs.

Finding a workable solution for such a woman is not simply a matter of brief counseling with respect to sexual behavior as such, but rather requires ongoing therapy for a considerable length of time, with the focus upon changing attitudes and outlook as she gradually gains tolerance of herself and others in a similar situation.

FEELING OF IDENTITY

Helping the newly divorced woman regain her sense of identity is one of the most important goals a counselor can have for his client. Too often married women lose their own identity as they lose their names. So Martha Crawford becomes Mrs. Harold Rothschild, wife of the new school superintendent. (Who ever heard of Mr. Martha Crawford?) When Ginny Krietmeyer married, she vanished, and in her place there was "Tom Duggan's pretty little wife" or "the druggist's wife." It is sad that marriage causes so many women to become mere shadows or extensions of their husbands, known because of what their husbands are, or what their husbands do or have. When the Duggans divorce, what happens to Tom Duggan's shadow? Who is she? She must establish her own feeling of identity which is built around her own view of herself as a person, the view others have of her, and the feedback she receives from them. She needs to become known for what *she* is and what *she* does. At first she may not quite know. Ginny Duggan was redecorating her living room, and discovered in counseling that she was, out of habit, choosing the type of furnishings she knew her ex-husband would have liked instead of the kind that she had almost forgotten she really wanted. Self-esteem, confidence in her ability to make decisions (even though they may turn out to be mistakes), and pride in her own individuality are part of the feeling of identity, which can be a fortunate by-product of divorce, that will help the divorcée in future adjustment whether she remains single or eventually remarries.

CHAPTER 6

UNDERSTANDING THE CHILD
OF DIVORCE

MARJORIE KAWIN TOOMIM*

WHAT IS LOST?

THE MOURNING PROCESS

HOW DOES THE CHILD DEFEND AGAINST LOSS?

THE CHILD of divorcing parents must cope with a multitude of losses. While on the surface it appears that he has lost only the easy availability of a parent, in fact he has lost much more. He has lost a basic psychosocial support system. His own dynamic structure has been molded by this system; the fibers of his being have been interwoven with those of his family members in a way which, if not altogether positive for growth, were at least familiar and in some sort of balance. With the dissolution of the structure, the child must now find new support systems.

The process of coping with loss is the same, whether the loss is of a person, a relationship, or a possession; whether the cause of loss is death, divorce, or a marked widening of psychosocial distance (Bowlby, 1961). Losses must be mourned in order to satisfactorily separate from a person or relationship and to allow new persons and relationships to fulfill one's needs.

*The author wishes to thank Lillian Freeman and Pamela Kawin for thir assistance in the preparation of this paper.

91

How the child copes with the loss and the mourning process is crucial to his future development. A certain level of ego-strength, psychic energy, and external support is necessary to carry the mourning process through to completion. Few children have the capacity for healthy mourning before the age of three and one-half to four years (Siggins, 1961). Few children of divorcing parents have the requisite external support at any age.

In divorce, the problem of accepting loss and properly mourning is complicated by the difficulty of discriminating the exact nature of the various losses. Even when the father deserts, his loss is not clear and the child may feel justified in hoping for his return, though, in fact, there is no hope.   *sometimes*

Divorce losses are difficult to discriminate. Parents compound the problem by ignoring or denying that such losses exist. Some parents are too absorbed in their own pain to help the child appropriately; some do not recognize the various losses, naively believing that only the person of the father is gone. Parents may even state that the child has not lost his father at all—or claim they will now have a better relationship because they will see more of each other. Where such denial of reality of loss occurs, the parent and the child cannot share mutual thoughts and feelings, or explore alternative ways of meeting needs together. The gap grows wider and losses mount. Parental failure to help in this trying time also alienates the child from himself. The child cannot cope with the overwhelming nature of his feelings. He defends against them. He denies, represses, withdraws, regresses, projects, detaches. He retains in fantasy what is not there in reality and he does not adequately deal with the loss.

Incomplete mourning leaves a reservoir of painful memories and feelings experienced as an undercurrent of depression. A rigid defense system guards against the awareness of ambivalence and pain and is a distorting screen through which subsequent realities are passed, misperceived, and misconstrued. The pain of the loss remains buried, occasionally surfacing when defenses are lowered or "reminders" of the loss transcend the defense barrier. Energy must constantly be expended to hide the pain. Distortion of reality creates difficulties in living; avoidance of stimuli which might bring the pain to the surface leads to a narrowing of life-space. Loss follows loss as the individual finds himself only partially alive, unable to partake of whole areas of existence. Energies bound in denying and avoiding the reality of loss and its associated pain are not available for use in positive growth and development.

Loss hurts; it leaves scars; it diverts one's life-course. Acceptance of loss provides freedom to explore other alternatives in life and to have other experiences. Denial of loss leaves a gaping hole that may only be covered over. There is constant fear of falling into the darkness below. Denial of loss leaves a vacuum in which no substitute relationship can flourish. Needs are left unsatisfied. The feeling of loss pervades one's life. Acceptance of loss and healthy, complete mourning provide a stable base for future growth.

Some of the trauma of divorce can be prevented by advance planning. Divorcing parents prepare themselves by a long period of questioning, expressing feelings, protesting and despairing, exploring alternatives in fantasy or in fact. Much of their mourning process is experienced in the context of the marriage. The child, on the other hand, is not prepared for this major change in his life. Furthermore, he must adjust to sudden loss in a chaotic family setting.

Parents need to respect the ways in which the child copes with divorce. His stress is great, his capacities limited. He does what he can to protect himself from what might be overwhelming stress. The parent may guide his adjustment patterns with tenderness and love, not with criticism and anger. The divorce adjustment takes years, during which time the dynamics need to be worked through repeatedly as the child's emotional strength and conceptual abilities mature. Young children almost universally deny some aspects of their situation. The aware parent can help the child integrate the realities the child brings to awareness as his strength grows. Insistence that the child see the whole reality at once will only bring resistance and move him further into denial and fantasy.

The following sections on "What is lost," "The mourning process," and "How the child defends against loss," describe in detail the complexities of divorce from the child's point of view. They are written to alert parents and counselors to interactions which often occur for children of divorce. With this knowledge and parental self-awareness the strain of divorce can be minimized. A good divorced family structure may even allow for growth not possible to attain in the failing marriage. They are not intended to deter parents from divorcing—only to help them enter into this new family relationship intelligently and with care. Divorce may be the most important event in your child's life.

WHAT IS LOST?

Loss of Faith and Trust

A tacit contract is entered into by parents upon the birth of a child. The parents, in effect, promise to establish a firm psychosocial base from which the child can grow. In return, he is expected to remain with the parents, to develop and mature. The child in a two-parent family generally expects that the parental unit will continue to be available to him until he no longer needs it. Most parents encourage this belief by assuring the child of their love, concern, and intention to maintain the family structure. Most parents, experiencing a strain in their relationship, are especially vocal in such reassurance hoping to allay his fears and "make him feel secure." They do not want him to be unnecessarily upset, just in case they are able to remain together.

For the child, it does not matter how unhappy the parents are together or how reasonable and right that they separate. He only sees that they have been unable to solve their problems in such a way as to maintain *his* security. Even where a parent is cruel or the strain in the relationship so great that divorce would ultimately benefit him, the child has no assurance that his lot will improve. He feels betrayed. He may feel so hurt that he never trusts again. The younger the child, the less he can understand, the more his need for both parents, and the more his need for a stable family unit, the more divorce will leave him feeling betrayed, angry, hurt and untrusting.

The hurt, untrusting child is in the uncomfortable position of needing help from parents who have just betrayed his trust. The likelihood of finding someone outside of the family to help him through this difficult time varies with the age of the child and his level of socialization. Very few children under six years of age have this ability. Beyond six, the willingness to ask for and receive help, the willingness of the parents to allow him to form a closer relationship with another adult or good friend, and the availability of a suitable, supportive individual are crucial factors.

Many children at this point deny their dependency needs and withdraw rather than trust either a parent or a parent-substitute. Or they may remain aware of unfulfilled dependency needs and feel helplessly angry. The child who remains aware of dependency needs and refuses to trust, places himself in the precarious interpersonal situation of feeling unsatisfied and of being unsatisfiable. He has laid the grounds within himself of a double-binding situation that may persist into adulthood where he simultaneously demands and rejects love. As a result, his needs remain unmet and he remains frustrated.

Parents are generally advised (Despert, 1962) not to distress their child unnecessarily by telling him of their difficulties before they separate just in case things can be "patched up." My experience with family crisis is that the child is aware of conflict but does not understand it. Mistrust grows in such an interpersonal setting. Parental honesty builds trust. Parents can be open about the seriousness of their difficulty without burdening the child with unnecessary details, fighting in his presence, or using him in their struggle. Rather, they can *talk about* the fact that they have problems and how they are trying to solve them. The child usually can understand the parents' situation if it is discussed in terms of the child's own difficulties with playmates. Care *must* be taken to understand the extent of his ability to deal with the details of the conflict.

The separation counseling model* provides an optimum situation in which the child can be prepared for divorce. Such an approach not only builds trust, but also provides the child with an effective model for conflict resolution. Even the concept that separation may be a constructive step in problem solving may help the child. Knowing when to end a relationship is a sign of strength and success, not of failure.

Maintaining open communication between parent and child helps to build his trust and provides a strong support for him. Only thus can the parents help the child cope with the many changes with which he will be faced as he grows in a divorced family. It is important that parents understand the child's experience of divorce, the logical and moral systems under which he operates at various developmental stages and the ways in which this particular child

*See Chapter 7, "Separation Counseling: A Structured Approach to Marital Crisis."

copes with stress. Without this understanding the parent runs a high risk of being misunderstood and rejected.

Respect for the child's attempts to cope with his difficulties will also increase parental availability and support. The child who feels accepted will be more likely to keep the parent informed of how he perceives the changes in his life and will ask for continued clarification of his thoughts and feelings. As the child develops, he is increasingly capable of conceptualizing and integrating the whole reality of divorce.

Loss of the Child-Mother-Father Relationship

In an intact family, the child has a child-mother relationship, a child-father relationship, and a child-parents relationship. Each parent gives him something; each provides a measure of support, control, nurturance, etc. Together they complement and supplement each other. Even parents in conflict represent a unit. In fact, they represent a very strong unit if, for example, the child has learned to use one as a rescuer when he displeases the other, or if he has learned to gratify his needs by using their divergence to manipulate.

Unless he has assumed a large portion of child care functions, the father of the infant from 0 to 18 months is more important for his role then for his person. The infant is primarily involved at the interpersonal level with his mother, especially in executing the difficult task of breaking his symbiotic bond with her and establishing his individuality (Mahler, 1971, McDevitt and Settlage, 1971). The father now represents a vital source of support for the mother, permitting her to give the child consistent care so that he may gradually learn to cope with separation according to his daily needs and capacity to tolerate stress. The father also represents a safe person the child can go to as he explores nonmother space. Relating to both father and mother gives him social skills necessary for complex interpersonal relationships.

After the child can hold images of absent people and objects in his mind (18 months or before), the loss of the father as an *individual* is increasingly important. Also, he grows more vulnerable to even brief separation from familiar people, places and things. Until he can maintain a sense of self when separated from his parents, especially his mother, he is particularly likely to be hurt by divorce. At least three years of stable mother-child relationship is required to complete the separation-individuation process successfully. Oedipal experiences of the three to five-year-old are difficult to work through in a disrupted family, and nonparental friends and lovers intensify the Oedipal crisis.

The child whose parents stay together during the vital period in which basic identification patterns are established will gain ego-strength. Even though parents differ markedly, the child is better able to take from each in an integrated way when they are together. It is also easier to talk about these differences with parents while they are together. Divorced parents seldom are able to talk about each other with good feeling, particularly when value and life-style differences are involved. As parents separate, differences tend to become accentuated and criticized. What the child perceives of his parents is then filtered through this screen of negativity. A parent may be so anxious to pass his value systems on to a child and mitigate the values of the other parent that he pushes too hard. Such an approach leaves the child confused and likely to reject the values of *both* parents.

The older the child, the less the difference between the parental value systems and the greater the parents' ability to treat each other with respect after divorce, the less serious will be the loss of the parental unit for the child. Maintenance of open communication between the parents minimizes the loss of the parent-unit for the child. As stepparents are added to the child's extended family, such open communication greatly aids his ability to integrate new relationships with their attendant value systems and changes in control and dependency patterns.

Loss of the Predivorce Mother

It is generally the custom for children of divorce to remain in their mother's custody. Therefore, we will conceptualize the child's changing relationship with his mother in these terms.

The divorcing mother is in the process of changing her life. She must cope with her own feelings of loss and anxiety. She must find alternative ways of satisfying the needs formerly met by her marriage. She may have to find or change work. She may begin to look for other interpersonal relationships. She probably needs to lower her socioeconomic level, which means she may become less giving of things that cost money while, simultaneously, she is giving less of her time and attention. The child then feels rejected. Conversely, a divorcing mother may change her relationship with her child by turning to him for need gratification. She may begin to spend too much time with him, to use him for her emotional support. This child feels smothered.

Many mothers at this time become quite inconsistent. Some quickly try to be "both mother and father," precipitously changing nurturance and control patterns rather than waiting for a new interpersonal balance to evolve. The mother, concerned with her own adjustment, is less available and less sensitive to the child, leaving him with more cause and opportunity to break rules. At the same time that she provides this latitude, the mother may be more punitive or harsh when she does realize that her limits have been violated. Or she may be more harsh because she must deal with control issues when she is overburdened by her own problems. She may then react to her own punitiveness by guilt and overconcern. She may become overpermissive and allow too much freedom because she feels guilty about the divorce or feels this kind of giving will make up for the child's loss. She may be just too overwhelmed by her own adjustment problems to expend her energies in child-control. That is something she can "always do later." Perhaps the school or a "Big Brother," or the "father-when-he-comes-over" will do it for her. She may use her energy to get a new husband-father who will assume the child-control function for her. Sulla Wolff (1969), discussing children of deceased fathers notes that adjustment was better when their homes were kept intact by mothers who were independent, hard-working, and energetic and who took on the working role with little conflict. Qualities of warmth and affection deemed of primary value for the married mother are less important for the separated mother. Mothers who clung to their children for support, especially their sons, impeded their maturation. Sons of such mothers tended to be tied to the mother and had difficulty establishing a good sexual adjustment.

Personal qualities of mothers may change a great deal as a result of divorce. Some mothers feel relieved at the resolution of their marital conflicts and thus are more relaxed with their children. However, if they become heavily involved in dating during this euphoric period their children feel deprived and rejected. Mothers who feel depressed and overburdened by the stress of divorce, though they stay home, are experienced as rejecting by their children. However the mother responds to divorce, the ways in which the child has learned to cope with her are no longer altogether satisfactory. Some change must be effected in order to function well with her again. In addition, the postdivorce child has different needs and so requires new maternal qualities and behaviors. Thus, predivorce reciprocal role relationships are lost, and postdivorce relationships must be established.

Children tend to idealize the predivorce mother and may try to cling to the fantasy that somehow they can get her to change back to her "old self." Feelings of guilt, inadequacy, frustration, and anger arise when they cannot. At times, they believe that the return of the predivorce mother will bring the father back. These manipulations of the postdivorce child serve only to create greater stress for the postdivorce mother. She thus becomes even more "different" than she was. The clinging child is further alienated.

A mother who is fairly stable emotionally, has a firm sense of values, and has established predivorce support systems for herself in addition to those provided by her husband and the marriage relationship, is less likely to change much within herself after divorce. She will, as a result, be more accessible to adapt to her child's changing needs.

If the father cannot provide for the family's support, the mother should establish a work pattern and child care facilities before separation. Thus, her stress is reduced at the time of divorce and the child is given an opportunity to cope with this change within the frame of an intact family. The mother who is unable to cope with the changes in her life comfortably should seek counseling. She thus minimizes the loss of the predivorce child-mother relationship.

Loss of the Predivorce Father

In a divorce in which the father leaves the home, the father-child relationship changes drastically and precipitously. In the ordinary family, the father works regularly, and thus is available to the child in a more limited and structured way than is the mother. After divorce, the structure becomes more rigid and highly limited in time and space. Thoughts and feelings the child may wish to communicate to the father or the sharing of activities must wait until the appointed time. And at that time, both the psychological and the physical space in which father and child meet are often not conducive to the delayed communication or activity. Maintaining a flowing, comfortable, in-depth relationship is ordinarily difficult for many fathers and their children; it is almost impossible under divorce conditions. Time with father is often time to be close "whether you feel like it or not." The closeness, if achieved, must be broken off at the appointed time or "Mommy will be mad" or "because Daddy has other plans for the evening." Many children will not open themselves to closeness under these conditions. Many will not tolerate the pain of repeated separation and loss. It is like reliving the divorce with each contact. Many children are fussy and angry with their mothers after a happy day with father.

On-going reciprocal role relationships between father and child are disrupted in the event of divorce where father leaves the home. The only roles that are traditionally given to the absent father are those of financial supporter, the giver of fun times and extra goodies, and the person who leads the child to much of the outside world through trips, talk of work or business, etc. If the father has held the traditional role of disciplinarian, he cannot do this well at the end of the week or over the phone. Also, he may be reluctant to discipline the child on his visiting day for fear of leaving the child with a bad feeling about him.

In the predivorce family with an active father, his authoritarian role contributes enormously to the ethical-moral value structure of the home. If the father has held the role of rescuer in mother-child struggles, his help will now be rejected by the mother as interference and side-taking unless she actually solicits it. The child may have difficulty accepting the father's help because of mixed feelings and divided loyalties. He may even use such help against the mother or accuse his father of trying to take him from the mother.

The father's role as provider of the masculine principle in the child's life is difficult to maintain on a limited contact. Visiting the child or going out to "have fun" can not replace the feeling that exists when a father actively lives in the home. This feeling is one of almost magical strength and protection against evil or powerful forces. It often transfers from the man to the child, even though by adult standards he might be considered weak and ineffectual. The concept of father as strong protector is further threatened by maternal criticism of the father. Also, the fact that the father does not return or is prevented by the mother from returning home and thus putting the child's world "right" again may be evidence to the child that he does not have the power to help at this important juncture in his life.

Biller's (1971) review of research studies of father-absent sons indicates that the loss of the father as a sex-role model has more effect on boys before the age of six than after. Father-absent boys tend to be less aggressive and less interested in sex-role stereotyped activities than are boys whose father remained in the home. However, the effects of father-absence on sex-role stereotyping may be mitigated by the mother's positive attitude toward the absent father and other males, and by her generally encouraging her boy's masculine behavior. Father-absence does not significantly affect the sex-role stereotyping of girls.

The continued availability of the postdivorce father in part determines how much is lost. However, the child's fantasy relationship with the father may be more significant than his actual presence. For example, an adolescent girl of sixteen had maintained constant contact with her father through wish-fulfilling day-dreams and fantasies since his desertion in her third year. The fantasies were reinforced by his monthly support check, one letter and one gift a year, and her mother's constant complaints about him. On the other hand, a twelve-year-old girl whose parents divorced when she was four and a half often refused to respond to his daily telephone calls and went with him Sundays only reluctantly at the mother's urging.

Father-absence in divorce is ambiguous. Unless he has deserted totally, he is clearly available to the child at some times. Children believe their fathers could make contact by phone or could come "if they really wanted to" or loved the child enough, etc. The postdivorce father is there-but-not-there. Such a frustrating situation predisposes the child to respond with father idealization and clinging or with resentful rejection.

Any action that minimizes the ambiguity of the postdivorce father's place in the child's life minimizes his loss. His new role must be clearly defined. Time commitments must be honored—even if the father sees the child irregularly, he will maintain the child's trust if he is clear about his availability. It is always better if the child and father work out their relationship together without maternal guidance. The mother's role is to accept and support whatever solution they reach.

Many children idealize their divorced fathers as a way of denying their loss (see below). Such idealization, though often hard for the mother to accept, needs to be respected. Both parents can assist the child in expressing and accepting ambivalent feelings. Tolerance for ambivalence is essential to perceiving the father as a whole person with both positive and negative qualities.

Loss of Environmental Supports

Many divorcing families move from one home to another. Such a move means the child will lose his familiar surroundings. Most children lose a special room in which was found safety, security, and refuge. Older, more socialized children lose friends, school, neighboring adults, perhaps youth organizations and leaders. Environmental supports become more meaningful as familiar parental supports disintegrate. Creating new supports at a time of stress, weakened ability to trust, and negative feelings about oneself is a difficult task. The effect of these losses can be disabling and should not be underestimated. Divorcing families should not move unless it is essential. If it is essential, staying in the same neighborhood reduces the loss.

The Loss of the Predivorce Child

The child, after family dissolution, is not the same as he was before. So pervasive are the changes in his intimate relationships and environmental supports that his feelings and perceptions of himself and others are profoundly affected.

Children are less secure after divorce. They question, with justification, parental ability to maintain a stable environment. They trust less. Dependency and control relationships become difficult. One of the major disruptions the child of divorce experiences is a discontinuity in identification. Before the divorce, he had been able to assimilate and integrate qualities from both parents with a reasonable degree of freedom. After divorce, the parents are realistically changed. In addition, the child perceives them differently. Generally one is idealized and the other depreciated. Furthermore, if parents criticize each other the child may be afraid to identify with qualities formerly deemed acceptable. With these changes in identification models, the child may now reject formerly acceptable parts of himself which are like a parent he now rejects. He may also experience conflicting feelings about qualities that are now unacceptable to one or the other parent because they are reminders of the divorced partner. Conversely, a child may purposely emulate the qualities of one parent to anger the other, or he may seek to become like the absent parent in order to keep the feeling of closeness. Such major identification shifts cause a changed, usually lowered, self-image.

Most children experience an unrealistic sense of guilt and responsibility about the divorce. This contributes to feelings of failure, inadequacy and lowered self-esteem. Before the age of seven, the child's view of justice is one of retribution. He believes anything bad that happens must be punishment for his wrong-doing. Parental quarrels must be about him; the divorce must be his fault. In addition, the child believes that if his parents loved him, they would reunite, therefore they don't love him. "Perhaps," he thinks, "I am unlovable. What did I do wrong?" The young child's omnipotent fantasies create a fear of his own power as well as an awareness of helplessness. This issue of power becomes central for the child whose parents divorce during his second through fourth year. At this age a thought is equivalent to action. To be angry with a parent, to wish him gone, and then to find him in fact gone is translated by the child into, "He left because I got angry." The situation is further complicated for the two- to four-year-old in that he often entertains destructive fantasies when frustrated. His inability to conceptualize future time and permanence leaves him the freedom to say "I'm going to chop you up" with little fear (Stone and Church, 1968). When, however, loss really occurs, he grows fearful of his anger and magic power. On the other hand, he finds himself powerless to right "his" wrong or to reunite his parents. For example, a thirteen-year-old girl whose parents divorced when she was four announced to her mother one day, "I guess I won't try to get you and Dad together again." This child had devoted nine years of her life to the accomplishment of an impossible task. She saw herself inadequate and a failure. Indeed, so much of her energy was directed to this hopeless project that she had not developed ego-skills necessary for effective functioning in the real world.

In addition to manipulating to reunite his parents, the child may play one against the other or express anger when, in fact, he feels intolerable fear and sadness; as a result he ends up rejecting parents who care for and love him. He may regress to lower levels of functioning to increase his security. He may feel guilt if his manipulations *are* successful. These manipulations often bring both parental and self-criticism. Thus a negative self-concept is reinforced by those on whom he depends, with whom he identifies, and by himself. The child who feels himself "bad" then clings to parents seeking reassurance that he is loved and wanted. Such reassurance from parents who are so deeply involved in the child's conflicting feelings and manipulations is seldom meaningful. They often serve only to reinforce his negative self-image.

The stability of the parent-child relationship is threatened by divorce. Before the age of seven, a child thinks in terms of authoritarian morality (Flavell, 1963, Wolff, 1969). Rules are sancrosanct and cannot be changed. What is right for one person must be right for all. Thus, it is not difficult to conceive that if it is right to divorce a parent, why is it not right to divorce a child? If one parent can reject the other for "breaking a rule" or being difficult to live with, why could not the child be rejected for exceeding some limit? He also stays out late, gets angry, likes someone besides mommy or daddy, etc. To tell the child he is not divorceable is difficult, for he has effectively been divorced by the parent who has left him. What assurance does he have that his remaining parent will not also leave? In socioeconomic settings where foster home or boarding school placement is common, such fears may be quite realistic.

A very complex group of feelings are associated with separation from a person on whom one has come to depend. A child must learn to cope with these feelings as he separates from the symbiotic mother-child relationship, from parents and friends as they come and go or from toys as they are lost. In an optimal growth situation short-term separations and minor losses are experienced in such ways that the child learns to deal with the attendant anxiety. Gradually, he learns to depend on his own resources for self-support. He learns to trust that those on whom he depends will be available when needed, even though they are not available all the time. The child from birth through the third year is constantly struggling with the task of separating. Even after this he remains vulnerable to devastation from major losses until he has developed sufficient ego-strength, self-confidence, interpersonal skills and support systems outside of the family to feel that he can survive if the parent is not physically available to help him cope with problems. This level of development seldom occurs before the sixth or seventh year. It may never develop for the child who comes from a strife-ridden home or who has been unable to adjust after overwhelming separations resulting from, for example, major illness, hospitalization or prolonged parental absence. Also, it may never develop if he perceived the birth of a sibling in terms of parental loss. Separation anxiety assails this weakened child at any age when traumatized by the flood of losses which accompany divorce.

Any separation evolves simultaneously a complex set of emotions. These include at minimum love, anger, fear, sadness, helplessness, hopelessness and—especially for children—guilt.

Love includes feelings of dependency, attachment and need. Without these feelings no loss would be experienced. Perceived abandonment, hurt, frustration of needs and wants satisfied by the lost person or relationship breed *anger*. *Fear* is experienced in terms of being alone; of further abandonment; of one's own vulnerability; of the possibility that one's own destructive powers may have been responsible for the loss. *Sadness*, the hallmark of loss, is the feeling when something of value has gone and can never be again, the sorrow from impoverishment of the self, the finality of an ending. *Helplessness* is the knowledge that one is not omnipotent; one did not have the power to prevent the loss. Life will continue without the lost person or relationship. *Hopelessness* is the acceptance of the reality and finality of the loss. Even if the lost person returns, it is never the same. The memory and experience of loss alters the relationship. The greatest problem for the postdivorce child is accepting the hopelessness of reinstating the family. *Guilt* usually accompanies loss, especially for the child who still believes he is all-powerful. Guilt is proportional to the perception of his responsibility for the loss, and for his wish that the loss would occur.

How the child copes with this complex set of emotions has a major effect on his subsequent development. The overwhelming force and confusion of these feelings is often too great and he turns them off. He detaches emotionally. Sometimes one of these emotions is more acceptable than the others and this one dominates when any of the others are felt. Thus, the first response to any emotional stimulus becomes anger or tears or fear or sometimes even love. A child can seldom deal with this complex of intense feelings alone. He needs parental support to allow their full expression as well as to gain tolerance for ambivalent feelings.

Parents can provide this support by sharing their own separation-related feelings with the child. This does not mean the parent should overwhelm the child with emotion. Rather, the parent can let the child know he also feels sad, sometimes scared, and sometimes glad about the divorce; angry and at the same time loving and needing; helpless and struggling; hopeless about the past and hopeful about a realistic future; guilty and simultaneously justified in separating; aware of everyone's pain.

The loss of inner security and sense of self-worth through divorce is the greatest loss of all. It is also the loss which can most easily be prevented, given parental awareness and skill in helping the child through this critical experience.

Divorcing parents should be particularly careful of the child two to seven years of age. He needs complete parenting and is unable to understand the complexities of divorce. After seven, the cognitive capacity to understand divorce, strength of identity and sense of autonomy, and supports in the outside world (friends, school), and inner supports (reading, etc.) increase with age. Least affected by divorce is the adolescent, for he is already in the process of separating from his parents.

Divorcing parents will best be able to help the child maintain a positive self-image if they accept the special ways he perceives and conceptualizes events in the outside world, his emotional capacities, and his defense patterns. Such accepting parents will be less reactive to divorce related manipulations, emotional outbursts, and defense maneuvers. The accepting parent can control himself and the child better, help him understand, accept himself, and guide him in ways which will build his self-image.

THE MOURNING PROCESS*

The fact that a child's parents divorce is much less important for his future development than for how he reacts to the experience. Does he perceive the divorce as a punishment? Does he find the experience overwhelming? Does he compliantly appear accepting while secretly he is angry and too afraid to express anger? Does he rebel openly? Does he manipulate to get his family back together? Does he also expect to be rejected? Does he recognize his losses and mourn them, or does he cover over the pain and leave an empty space inside?

The healthy mourning process involves:

a. Accepting the reality of the loss.

b. Experiencing fully and accepting the complex feelings which are always associated with loss (love, anger, fear, sadness, helplessness, hopelessness and sometimes guilt).

c. Finishing "unfinished business" associated with the loss, i.e., resolving ambivalent feelings, expectations, disappointments, things left unsaid or undone, etc. (Tobin, 1971).

d. Gradually releasing the lost person or relationship. This may be accomplished in active involvement with the separating person if open contact can be maintained. Where loss is sudden and contact is lost, introjecting the lost one or maintaining a fantasy relationship with him gives the mourner time to master the experience. Ties are then gradually cut while strength develops and alternative ways to gratify needs are explored.

e. Establishing new ways to gratify needs.

How Can the Child Be Helped to Complete the Mourning Process?

Acceptance is the essence of healthy mourning. Parents can help

*For full discussion of the healthy mourning process see Bowlby, 1961; Fenichel, 1945; Jacobsen, 1971; Volkan and Showalter, 1968.

the child by accepting their own loss and their own loss-associated feelings. The separation process is essentially the same for all members of the family, even though the specific losses differ. The more deeply the parents explore and understand themselves, the better they will understand and support their child. When both parents address their attention to this process, they form a parent-unit for the child. Such a unit mitigates the loss of the child-mother-father unit of the married family.

The parent will help most by focusing on the reality of the child's feelings about his many losses; these are the most immediate in the awareness of everyone concerned. Feelings may be indirectly expressed, but a parent who is in touch with his own emotional experience will be likely to attend to the underlying "real" feeling. Thus, for example, a child who is fussy after a good day with his father is probably sad and defends against this feeling with anger. It does little good to *ask* a young child what he feels, for he has limited ability to put his deep feelings into words. The empathic parent can look at the child's body, his behavior, and his external situation and make some guess about the child's feelings. In this situation a mother might say:

Mother: You looked sad as you came in—before you got angry with me. Did something special happen that made you feel bad?

Child: Oh . . . No . . . We went to the zoo and had chocolate ice cream.

Mo: It must be hard for you to have fun with Dad and then have to leave him. I sometimes feel sad after we have a nice phone conversation. I wish then we could have stayed together. Then I get angry because we couldn't. I almost wish sometimes we didn't have the good times, because I feel lonelier when they are over.

Ch: Why can't Daddy come in the house with me when he brings me home?

Mo: Oh. I didn't realize that was important to you.

Ch: Well, I asked him to tuck me in bed like he used to, and he said he couldn't come in the house with me.

Mo: I will talk to him about that tomorrow and see what we can do. I can understand that you would like him to tuck you in. It really feels good to have a Daddy do that, doesn't it. If you will accept a substitute, I would like to tuck you in tonight while you tell me about the zoo.

By thus focusing on underlying feelings, the child brought to the foreground one of the losses which was important for him, the tuck-in ritual with daddy. He was able to express his anger about the loss of this child-father interaction. He acted out his ambivalence. It was accepted and a resolution offered. We may assume he felt a sense of rational control over his life and accepted a substitute need—satisfied for the evening. He may also have trusted his parents would work together to give him at least a symbol of something important to him. A fight was avoided and support was given at a crucial time. The child accepted his own needs and feelings as well as effective mothering. Had the mother reacted with anger to his anger, he would have felt less trusting of her sensitivity and caring for him. He would have felt guilty, angry, and afraid at a time when he was especially needy and sad. He probably would have gone to bed pouting, brought his mother back to him with numerous demands (water, blankets, another story, etc.). Perhaps he would have had a nightmare and come to her to relieve his fear.

This issue could have been handled by his father directly. As it was, his mother had to accept the responsibility for dealing with the problem. The father had reinforced his own idealized image as all-giving but failed to deal with the whole child. The following type of father-child interaction would have been appropriate:

Child: Will you come in and tuck me in tonight? You haven't done that for such a long time.

Father: I'd really like that but I don't feel comfortable in the house any more.

Ch: But it is still your house. Besides, you told me you were just divorcing mother, that you were not divorcing me. I want you to come in and tuck me in tonight.

Fa: Wait a minute. There are about three things going on here. Let's get them straight. First of all, I guess you want me to spend more time with you, or do something that would feel close for both of us. You thought about my tucking you in as a way of doing that. Second, you brought up the whole issue of the divorce and my place in the house and the family now. Third, you became demanding and angry, and I started to get mad about being forced to do something for you.

Ch: OK. Forget it.

Fa: No, I don't want to forget it. Let's try to work it out. I miss the things we used to do together that just came easily when I was living in the house, like putting you to bed or reading with you or watching TV. I enjoy our Sundays and the zoo was fun, but we don't have much opportunity to just be quiet together. And you and Mommy and I are never together as a family.

Ch: The house isn't much fun without you. Mommy is always tired and busy now. And she has that other guy here all the time. If she marries him, you can't ever come back.

Fa: Oh, did your wanting me to come in the house have something to do with wanting me to come back to live there?

Ch: Well, will you?

Fa: No, I won't come back. Mommy and I have found that we are much better off living apart, I know it hurts you and that both Mommy and I lose a lot in our relationship with you. But I also remember how much we used to fight and how afraid you were that we might hurt each other. We weren't very good for you that way, either.

Ch: I don't remember the fights very much any more, just the good times. Mommy talks about the fights, but I don't like to listen to her when she does that. She tries to take me away from you. She doesn't want me to like you.

Fa: I can't say what Mommy wants or is trying to do. I think Mommy and I had better get together and work out more of our differences. It sounds as though you are being put in the middle between us, and I don't like to see that. I will call Mommy in the morning.

Ch: OK. But what about tonight?

Fa: Well, I will go to the door and see if Mommy would object to my putting you to bed tonight. But, I don't think that will solve the whole problem. Next week let's go to my apartment and have a regular "Sunday at home" instead of doing something special.

Ch: Could I invite a friend to come along?

Fa: Sure. Now I'll go and talk to Mom.

In this interaction, the father was able to set limits on the child. He shared his feelings of loss; he took responsibility for the divorce with his wife, and relieved the child of the pressure of trying to reunite the family. He took an active role in the family interaction and understood the child's need for closeness with him in a less formal arrangement. The request that a friend join them for the "day at home" is indicative of conflicting feelings about such intimacy. It appears that his child holds unrepressed resentment toward him. He would do well to arrange to wrestle with this child during his day at home, or find some other activity that will allow for expression of ambivalent feelings.

By interactions such as the one noted above, communication paths are maintained, trust is built, losses for the child are clarified and defined. The defined loss can be accepted, and substitute gratifications found. Hundreds, perhaps thousands of such interactions are required to accomplish the task of complete divorce mourning. It must be done over and over again.

It is important to recognize that divorce losses change as the child develops. For example, parents who remain so estranged that the father is not allowed in the house will create discomfort for the child at all special events throughout his life where families come together (birthdays, graduations, weddings, etc.). He loses his fantasy of family unity at each of these events.

It is to be hoped that effective parent-child interactions will teach the child to cope with each loss successfully as it comes to awareness. In time he will need parental support only when he is so confused that he cannot sort out the issues himself.

All of us defend against loss because it is overwhelming. Parents must respect the child's perception of his own strength and only help him confront reality when he shows readiness to accept help, much as sexual information is gradually given. He will turn away or misperceive what is said to him if he feels he cannot absorb the reality.

The child needs to finish "unfinished business" with his parents and confront his feelings about them in the present (Perls, 1969; Tobin, 1971). It must be remembered that there are actually great changes in the parents as well as the child as a result of the divorce. Children need to work through their "unfinished business" with the predivorce parents in the context of how he was then as well as how he is now. The following example illustrates this point:

Ch: Mom—why don't you ever cook any more?

Mo: I do cook—I make dinner and breakfast and fix your school lunches.

Ch: But I remember you used to be cooking every day when I got home from school. You made cookies and cakes and things.

Mo: Oh that was before the divorce. Now I am at work when you come home from school.

Ch: That is how I always think of you in the kitchen when I came home from school. I liked the good smells and helping you.

Mo: Sounds like you really miss that part of me.

Ch: Yes. Like you aren't my mother now, 'cause my mother was always in the kitchen when I got home from school.

Mo: You sound sad—like you really lost me.

Ch: I am sad— (child hits the sink).

Mo: Are you angry, too?

Ch: Well—it's not your fault and you had to work.

Mo: No, it's not my fault, but you can still be angry that I don't have time to bake now and that you feel like you lost your mother.

Ch: I don't feel right getting mad at you. You do so much now. I mean, you work so hard.

Mo: Are you feeling that I work so hard that you don't get enough mothering now? Like you are deserted now?

Ch: Well, it would be nice if we could have more fun? You are always so tired, now.

Mo: I miss the good times we had, too. I remember now that we used to talk a lot when you came home from school. You told me about what you did and I liked baking with you. I have lost touch with that part of you. When I cook dinner now, you are watching TV and I am so rushed to put dinner on the table I don't cook the same things. I remember now that you would chop things for me and stir things that took time. Now I use a lot of frozen food. Asking you to set the table is a lot different from asking you to cook with me. No wonder you resent setting the table now and you didn't before.

Ch: I didn't realize the difference either. And I can't talk to you about my stuff anymore. At dinner now you always answer the phone because it might be a date calling. (Ch. looks away and starts to move away.)

Mo: (Moving toward the child) I feel sad, too. I don't want to lose you in all the changes that have happened since the divorce. Let's sit down now and see how we can get back some of the good things we have had together. Would you sit on my lap for a while?

Ch: Nods assent and starts to cry.

Too much was brought forth in this interaction to be dealt with at the moment. Sadness, anger, and love were the dominant emotions. The anger was directed both at the mother and at her "dates."

In a therapeutic setting, the child ideally would have hit some mother-symbol (pillow, chair) while the mother held the child so that the complex of feelings, love, anger, hopelessness, etc., could have emerged together. After the feelings had been expressed, the two could more easily find the closeness they once had. Some mothers would be able to cope with such an interaction outside of a therapeutic setting. Mother and child together would mourn the irretrievable loss of the mother-in-the-kitchen-when-I-come-home-from-school ritual, and find another mutually satisfying activity that would allow two-way open communication. The child would also, at some time, deal with feelings of resentment toward the mother's suitors, and the mother's tiredness and general unavailability. The child's present needs would be assessed. There may be something particularly difficult to discuss at this time which would have been easier to bring up in the earlier "kitchen" setting. Or, if the time between the remembered interaction and the present is very long, perhaps the child needs some way to regress as a defense against a present stress. The conflict between anger engendered by frustrated needs for mothering, and guilt or overconcern about her mother's additional burdens could be explored. No feelings are expressed in the above interaction about either the divorce or the father. Interventions that might have been appropriate include: "If Dad were here, then things would be the same as they used to be." "Sometimes I wish we had never divorced. Things would be easier then." "Even if Dad were still here, I had planned to go to work at this time." Also, no mention was made of possible changes in the child's situation. For example: "Then we were so far from people, you had no one to play with. Now we live in a neighborhood with lots of children and you play after school." "You seemed frightened then, and hung on me a lot. Now you seem to be having more fun with friends. Is that right?"

HOW DOES THE CHILD DEFEND AGAINST LOSS?

Dominant in the constellation of defenses of the child who cannot mourn his losses is either premature detachment or internalization of the lost one or some combination of these.

Premature Detachment (Bowlby, 1961, Deutsch, 1937, Heinicke, 1965) is evidenced by passive withdrawal, active rejection of the lost parent, unusually strong attachment to a substitute, loss of emotionality, or sudden denial of need for the lost relationship. Premature detachment involves a gross distortion of reality—either of the loss itself, or of the child's need for the lost one. Detachment almost always involves a splitting off of intense emotions. It is the most deceptive system, in that parents so easily overlook the child's underlying pain and react to him as if he were not hurt. Communication is thus blocked and the parents—even assuming they are willing and able to help the child—cannot help. What they do say and do is not addressed to the child's pain and thus he finds it irrelevant and frustrating. He concludes—properly—that his parents do not understand him, and so he further detaches himself from what parenting is available. He grows increasingly isolated and lonely.

The only positive aspect of this defense is that the child saves himself from what he perceives as an overwhelming experience. For him, this is a survival maneuver. Indeed, with it he can encapsulate his pain and deal with it at a later time when his ego is stronger and his support system more secure. Thus, we find adults in therapy working through long-buried thoughts and feelings associated with childhood loss (Volkan, et al., 1968).

In rejecting the lost parent, the child may also reject those qualities in himself that are like the parent. Such detachment from oneself weakens the child's ego, results in loss of self-esteem and self-awareness, and produces a poor base on which to grow. Some children choose to pattern themselves in any way *but* like the separated parent (develop a negative identification), and thus severely limit growth potential.

Premature detachment from a separated father is likely to result in a too-close relationship to the mother, providing she is available and nurturing. If she is not, the child may detach from her also, continuing to grow virtually parentless.

Parents of children who so defend themselves feel relieved, naively believing that they have easily adjusted. Only some years later do they realize that the child is disturbed and may trace the difficulty back to the time of divorce. The deceptively benign quality of premature detachment is illustrated by the following cases:

> Betty was four when her parents obtained an amicable divorce. She was told her father preferred to live away from home because it was better for his work. She saw him every Sunday. Normally bright and inquisitive, she asked few questions about the change in her family, was easily satisfied by superficial answers, and made no protest about the loss. Apparently she enjoyed the times with her father. He was rather a quiet man who liked to take her to interesting places. She had little difficulty separating from him when he brought her home and she hardly mentioned him between visits. Apparently not concerned about leaving her father when she left the country with her mother at the age of eight, she was quite disturbed about leaving her cat. Her relationship with her mother is close and not lacking in emotionality though anger has not been acceptable in her family. She functions well at school, has few friends. She now suffers from night terrors.

> Mrs. I. at forty has difficulties forming dependency relationships. After her parents divorced when she was seven, she seldom saw her father. Though she remembers their postdivorce relationship clearly, she has almost entirely forgotten their earlier relationship. She is told her predivorce relationship with him was very close. He was a "good" father to her. She has few predivorce memories of him. She clearly remembers an "embarrassing lack of feeling" when she realized he left home. In later years she came to resent his abandonment, particularly when she was unhappy with her mother. She dislikes those qualities in herself that resemble his. She has difficulty calling him "Daddy," but easily refers to him as "My Father." She abhors men who are like her view of her postdivorce father. She is attracted to men who are like her fantasy of her predivorce father, though she cannot form a lasting relationship with them. After the divorce, when her mother

had to go to work, she became quite self-sufficient and absorbed in school work. She became outwardly compliant and inwardly rebellious. Her present rigidly independent stance is a defense against her fear of dependency. She trusts nobody, including herself.

The opposite extreme of premature detachment is *internalization* of the person with the aim of circumventing loss. Internalization may be accomplished by holding a fantasy image of the person or relationship identifying with him (Krupp, 1954) or introjecting all or parts of him (Perls, 1969). At the extreme he may act as if he is the lost person (Deutsch, 1937). The child who internalizes the lost parent accepts the fact of loss but refuses to allow a new relationship to emerge. He maintains control in a fantasy relationship where in reality his control is strictly limited. He continually hopes for something that cannot be. He thus feels frustrated and angry. Underlying his outward appearance of control is his inner awareness of reality and his actual helpless, hopeless position. Internalization of the whole person with both positive and negative qualities is rare. Few children possess tolerance for inconsistency and ambivalence. Therefore, they retain only selected parts that fit a negative or positive image.

Internalization of negative qualities is more likely to occur if the predivorce father was feared. The child then gains power and relieves his own fear. A boy, particularly, may internalize his father's sex-role stereotyped behavior in order to resolve conflicts about his own masculinity. If he is not compatible with his mother, he may accentuate his father's negative qualities as a way of punishing her. He may "become" his father to be sent away like his father. Perhaps he takes on his negative qualities in order to force transfer of his custody to the father. Thus he avoids experiencing the guilt involved in actively rejecting his mother.

Internalization of the negative qualities of a parent lead to feelings of insecurity, anxiety, ambivalence, and poor self-image. The child comes to perceive himself as "negative" just as he did the lost parent. In addition, reactions of others to him are more likely to be negative and thus his self-image is further devalued and his tendency to be fearful, angry, and defensive is increased.

It appears that most children *internalize an idealized positive image* of a separated father, even though he has been cruel or negligent. I recently asked ten adolescent and adult clients from divorced homes:

How did maintaining an idealized father-image help you? The replies may be categorized as follows:

1. A denial of the loss:

   "I could not accept the fact that we would not be together anymore, so I kept him with me all the time. He was like an imaginery companion." "No one so good could have done such a terrible thing as to leave me, so this way I could pretend it was just temporary and he would be back." "I felt I needed a father, I emphasized the parts of him that I wanted in a father and kept him in my mind that way." "I kept them in my mind as together and happy. That way I didn't have to see them apart. I wanted to have a mother-father unit."

2. A source of support:

   "It really feels good to know that someone always loves you, even if he is 3000 miles away and you only see him once a year." "He was like a Prince Charming who was coming to rescue me." "I kept hope alive by thinking of him as loving and wanting me." "I felt I always had a haven to turn to—a place to go if things got too bad. Of course, I never tested to find out if he would have had me. Now I can see that he would not have wanted me." "Whenever I had a problem I couldn't solve, I would go to my room and have a fantasy in which he came to me and we talked. I did that until I was sixteen—that is the first time I saw him since I was three. Then, after I saw him, it wasn't so easy because he wasn't like my fantasy. I really felt I had lost something." "I didn't like my mother. This way I had at least one good parent."

3. A boost to self-esteem:

   "I must be OK if someone so nice cares about me." "No one wants to come from bad parents." "When my mother criticized me, I could keep from hearing her by thinking about my father and that at least he really cares so I must not be so bad." "Everybody else had a father. I wanted one too. And mine was better than theirs." "It was like he never left me, so I didn't have to feel guilty about their divorce." "I didn't like myself as a person who thinks bad things about people, especially my father."

4. An identification model:

   "I was afraid that if I carried around a bad image of him, I would get to be like that. So I kept him 'good'." "I guess I decided what kind of a father I wanted to have, and thought of him that way and then I identified with that image of him." "I don't understand how I got to be so much like him, since I only saw him a few times a year. Well, I am really more like the way I used to imagine him all the time, not the way I see him now." "I didn't like my mother and I didn't want to be like her, so I purposely imitated the good parts of him." "My mother kept telling me I was just like my father. She meant selfish, I didn't want to believe that, so I kept thinking about the good parts of him to be like."

The child who so idealizes the father may considerably distort reality. For example, one girl whose parents divorced when she was four and a half often talked about the "tradition" she and her father had of eating breakfast together every morning. Actually, the father never woke up before noon and seldom talked to her at all. Her mother's attempts to "help the child to see reality" were met with considerable resistance. Already viewing her mother as a rejecting person (the divorcer) and as denying her what she wanted, she became increasingly convinced of her mother's "badness" and her father's "goodness." She then clung even more tenaciously to the relationship with her still-distant father. With so little support for her idealized image in reality, she lived more and more in fantasy.

The child who idealizes his father often finds himself at cross-purposes with his mother. The mother wants to let the father go; the child wants to keep him. She is uncomfortable with the father's qualities; he accentuates them. The child may become unacceptable to the mother both as a mate symbol and realistically as a difficult child. The child may define qualities which are questionable as "good." For example, the child may idealize a father's spend-thrift qualities (through which he gets "goodies") and strain the mother's limited resources, clash with her value system, and create distance between mother and child by excessive demands for "things."

The most positive aspect of introjection of the idealized image of the lost parent is that the child takes control of satisfying his own support needs when his parents deny him such support. He refuses to be a helpless victim. Furthermore, he surrounds himself with a warm, loving, caring fantasy. He protects himself until he feels strong enough to accept the more harsh reality.

Problems with this defense arise primarily when the ideal and the real father obviously differ considerably. Contrast, for example, the case of the girl who maintained a fantasy relationship for thirteen years with a father who deserted her when she was three. She had full control of the fantasy relationship and was only frustrated when her mother faced her with "reality." She had the equivalent to a fantasy playmate or a relationship with Santa Claus. At the other extreme is the case of a girl who saw her father as all-loving and caring and then waited each week for his inconsistent Sunday visit. She often felt betrayed, frustrated, angry, sad, and frightened. She had to repress these feelings in order to maintain her fantasy. The negative feelings were instead turned against her mother, who expressed her resentment at the father's lack of concern.

The child's idealization of the father is the defense most disturbing to the mother. This is particularly true if her own ambivalent feelings are resolved by focusing on her husband's negative qualities (Toomim, 1972).

We may assume that the child himself, while holding onto and becoming like the father, is aware that father was unacceptable. To be like father may threaten his security with his mother. This is particularly true for the child who is told he is "just like his father."

It is difficult for a young child to conceive that parents who are different from each other and who reject each other can both be "good." Therefore, if the father is perceived "good" the mother is likely to be cast in the "not good" position. Parental attempts to manipulate the child's loyalty, change custody, get more or give less money, and to communicate with each other through the child, serve to increase his tendency to perceive one good and the other bad. The roles the divorced parents play also support a dichotomized view. The visiting father takes the child places, goes out for dinner with him, makes up for less time by more gifts and generally sees him only when he wants to and in a relatively good mood. Only the "best" of the visiting father is visible. The mother, on the other hand, increases her role as disciplinarian and has less money to spend than she had when the family was intact. She interacts with the child even when she is tired from working or upset from relationships with other men. She may be seen as rejecting when she pursues her own interests. She is often burdened by her role as single parent. In addition, she is usually perceived as rejecting or inadequate. The child believes she could have kept Daddy home "If she were better" or "If she wanted to."

Paradoxically, the mother is also a safer person to see as bad, even though rejecting her threatens the child's basic security. The father cannot be taken for granted. He is obviously able to leave and his life is complete in many ways without the child. The child must actively maintain the relationship with him. The child-mother relationship on the other hand is more stable. She has chosen to keep the child, may even have fought for him. Whether she is actually a "good" or a "bad" mother, she is a consistent external support who, by her role, gives him many opportunities to channel his confused feelings and gain a sense of mastery over his pain by struggling with her. He wants his idealized father but she is there. He wants his needs met by him; he accepts need-gratification from her. Father abandons him weekly; Mother stays—and her presence keeps Father away and thus frustrates the child. It is difficult to express anger to a now-giving father; easy to be angry with a controlling mother. However he expresses his distress—through anger, withdrawal, projection, etc.— the person who will be most involved in coping with the distress behavior will be the mother. Her natural reaction to the child's distress may be critical and thus unsupportive. In her own stress, she may not be aware of the child's deeper needs for security, understanding of his confused feelings, and relief from pain. His distress is generally frustrating to her. Her natural reaction then is likely to further alienate him from her at a time when he needs her most. He is now very likely to react by clinging to her with fear and anger while she reassures him. Still full of hurt and righteous indignation, his ambivalent feelings for her grow and his security is threatened by this interaction.

How Can the Parent Deal With the Child's Defense Behavior?

How the parent deals with the child's defense against the pain of loss is crucial. Confronting the defensive behavior directly tends to make the child *more* defensive. Criticizing his behavior or forcing him to "see reality" will strengthen the defense structure and build his conflictive and negative self-concept. He will turn against his mother and make meaningful communication with her almost impossible. Yet, it is important that the child accept the reality of his situation. Only as he accepts reality will he be able to effectively integrate his experience and his feelings regarding his changing family and self.

The way in which parents help their children cope with the complexities of divorce changes with the child's age. Children too young to express themselves verbally can be approached through play materials. For example, clay can be used to create a variety of family interactions with an unlimited number of characters. Clay also has the advantage of following the young child, who resists directly confronting his divorce trauma, to deal with it indirectly in third person terms.

Doll play, "dress-up," and role-playing are also good ways of helping the young child work through his feelings of loss.* Snapshots of predivorce family life may be compiled into a picture story which can be read repeatedly to keep real memories alive and in perspective. Postdivorce pictures from both parent lines may also be kept to help integrate the changing relationships that occur as he grows—perhaps as parents find other mates. Take pictures of homes, "special" places, toys, friends, ordinary as well as special events, and of course family members. Poses should be natural, not just smiling. This "picture history" gives the child an opportunity to face "reality" as if, and when, he is ready. It reduces his sense of loss.

Finding substitute need-gratification is a highly personal task. The parent can help explore alternatives; only the child can know what alternative will be acceptable. Many parents mistakenly believe a stepparent will replace a natural parent. For many children a stepparent represents a further loss. He may perceive the stepparent as a rival for his natural parents' time and attention; the stepparent may seem to be an intruder into his relationship with his own parents; the new values and new interpersonal structure threatens old accepted and cherished ways. New stepchildren further erode existing family systems. The problem of integrating such an extended family is a major one.

There is a delicate balance between respecting the child's need to defend against painful reality and helping him confront reality when he is ready. Both parents must work together and with the child to help him see reality as he becomes capable of coping with it.

Divorce never eliminates a parent. It only changes the family structure. For better or for worse a child never loses a parent totally. He has absorbed—introjected—a part of that parent which will always remain with him whether he keeps a fantasy image of him or a real one.

---

*For more details on play therapy and techniques see Virginia Axline, *Play Therapy* and also *Dibs, in Search of Self*.

I have focused attention on the basic issue of loss from the viewpoint of the child of divorce. No mention has been made of the child who stays with his father or of the influence of siblings. Too little has been said of the effect of mental age and social maturity and of the quality of parent-parent and parent-child relationships as vital factors affecting the child's divorce adjustment. Unfortunately I know of no research which explores these variables. My hope is that the concepts expressed in this paper will stimulate studies which point the way to effective counseling for children of divorce.

REFERENCES

Axline, V.: *Dibs, In Search of Self*. New York, Ballantine Books, 1964.

————: *Play Therapy*. New York, Ballantine Books, 1969.

Biller, H.: Father absence and the personality development of the male child. In *Annual Progress in Child Psychiatry and Child Development*. New York, Brunner, Mazel, 1971.

Bowlby, J.: Process of mourning. *Int J Psychanal*, 42:317-340, 1961.

————: Grief and mourning in infancy and early childhood. *Psychoanal Study Child*, 15:6052, 1960.

Despert, L.: *Children of Divorce*. New York, Dolphin Books, 1962.

Deutsch, H.: Absence of grief. *Psychoanal Q*, 6:12-22, 1937.

Fenichel, O.: *The Psychoanalytic Theory of Neurosis*. New York, W.W. Norton and Co., 1945.

Flavell, J.: *The Developmental Psychology of Jean Piaget*. New York, Van Nostrand Co., Inc., 1963.

Heinicke, C.: *Brief Separations*. New York, International Universities Press, Inc., 1965.

Jacobson, E.: *Depression*. New York, International Universities Press, Inc., 1971.

Krupp, G.: Indentification as a defense against anxiety in coping with loss. *Int J Psychoanal*, 46:303-314, 1965.

McDevitt, J. and Settlage, C.: *Separation-Individuation*. New York, International Universities Press, Inc., 1971.

Mahler, S.: How the child separates from the mother. In *The Mental Health of the Child*. Rockville, Md., National Institute of Mental Health, 1971.

Perls, F.: *Ego, Hunger and Aggression*. New York, Random House, 1968.

————: *Gestalt Therapy Verbatim*. Ogden, Utah, Real People, 1969.

Siggin, L.: Mourning: A critical review of the literature. *Int J Psychoanal*, 17:14025, 1963.

Stone, J.L. and Church, J.: *Childhood and Adolescence*. New York, Random House, 1968.

Tobin, S.: Saying goodbye in gestalt therapy. *Psychotherapy*, 8:150-155, 1971.

Toomim, M.: Structured separation with counseling: A therapeutic approach for couples in conflict. *Fam Process,* 11:299-310, 1972.

Volkan, V.: Normal and pathological grief reactions—a guide for the family physician. *Va Med Month,* 93:651-656, 1966.

————: Typical findings in pathological grief. *Psychiat Q,* 44:231-250, 1970.

Volkan, V. and Showalter, C.: Known object loss, disturbance in reality testing and "re-grief" work as a method of brief psychotherapy. *Psychiat Q,* 42:358-374, 1968.

Wolff, S.: *Children Under Stress.* London, Penguin Press, 1969.

CHAPTER 7

SEPARATION COUNSELING: A STRUCTURED APPROACH TO MARITAL CRISIS*

MARJORIE KAWIN TOOMIM

▬ ▬ ▬ ▲ ▬ ▲ ▬ ▲ ▬ ▲ ▬ ▲ ▬ ▲ ▬ ▲ ▬ ▲ ▬

RATIONALE FOR STRUCTURED SEPARATION WITH
   COUNSELING

THE SEPARATION STRUCTURE

SEPARATION COUNSELING

▲ ▬ ▲ ▬ ▲ ▬ ▲ ▬ ▲ ▬ ▲ ▬ ▲ ▬ ▲ ▬ ▲ ▬ ▲

MARRIAGE COUNSELORS and psychotherapists are all too familiar with the couple who come for help stating they must either "make this marriage work or get a divorce." One partner is generally inclined to cling desperately to the marriage, willing to do almost anything to avoid divorce. The other is desirous of the marriage, but tired of trying and sees no way to go but "out." Trial separation is generally not considered a reasonable alternative. The more threatened of the two is usually afraid to let go of the semblance of control available through physical proximity. The other is looking toward complete freedom. Both may have little tolerance for the lack of structure which is implied by separation as opposed to divorce. This paper presents a fourth alternative: a moderately structured, time-limited period of separation with counseling.

*This is an expanded version of a paper entitled, Structured Separation with Counseling: A therapeutic approach for couples in conflict, *Family Process*, *11*:299-310, 1972.

RATIONALE FOR STRUCTURED SEPARATION
WITH COUNSELING

Separation counseling is a form of crisis intervention counseling (Parad, 1965). It is a time-limited approach which deals specifically with the immediate crisis of family separation. The purpose of this counseling procedure is to help separating individuals understand their relationship, resolve their conflicts, decide whether their future relationship will be together or apart, and grow through the separation process.

A major assumption on which separation counseling is based is that a meaningful relationship, once established, can never be altogether lost. It can only be changed. In some cases, especially where there are children, separated partners continue to see each other and make decisions together. If they do not continue to have some tangible connection with each other, they nonetheless continue to relate to each other in fantasy, imagination and memory. It is important that the couple work through the separation process carefully and thoroughly so that little unfinished business remains to interfere with their continuing separation-relationship or in new relationships.

The techniques and methods outlined below are of particular value to separating couples, married or unmarried, and to parents and children who are separating. They may be applied by individuals with or without counseling. However, counseling is especially useful for couples having much difficulty separating, for extremely dependent individuals who are limited in emotional freedom, for those who are afraid to risk, and for those subject to severe depression.

The structured separation provides a firm time-space base within which individuals may maximize their freedom to experience and grow. It minimizes the shock of separation. It makes positive use of the separation process as an aid to development so that individuals neither deny their loss or become victims to its pain. Respect for self and other, trust, choice, courage, honesty, emotional development, and positive growth are inherent in this method.

Conflict-laden couples who choose to separate voluntarily before their discomfort becomes intolerable gain much from openly and consciously making this choice. Manipulative and punitive maneuvers such as capricious sexual behavior, designed to force a break in the relationship are avoided. Such maneuvers often cause irreparable damage, shatter trust, and humiliate one or both mates. In separating voluntarily, the partners signify that each values himself, the other, and what they have between them enough to allow some distance. Such distance provides each with an opportunity to gain perspective and to try alternative solutions to problems. The couple may then come together again with renewed understanding and feeling, or go on to other relationships having learned a great deal from this one. Separation counseling insures that little unfinished business remains to interfere with new experiences.

Structured separation is an excellent model for distressed families with children. These children are thus presented with parental behavior where honesty, choice, and respect are primary values. Some of the damage done by the suddenness and emotional uproar common in most divorce is mitigated. The children have both time and an open interpersonal situation in which to adapt to this major change in their lives. The children have an opportunity to discuss their feelings about the family as it has been and as they would like it to be. Their sense of involvement and control of their fate is considerably increased. Children's positive feelings for their parents are enhanced by seeing them cope well with conflict and crisis. In addition, parents experience less anxiety in this structured separation situation than in a comparable time negotiating for a final divorce. They thus are able to deal with their children's feelings more effectively. The separation counselor has an opportunity to help parents understand their children's reactions to the family crisis. He may then guide the parents so that they can encourage open exchange of feelings and concerns. Where necessary, the counselor may work directly with the children.

Viable relationships survive structured separation. Old patterns of thought, feeling, and behavior are broken. New patterns develop within each individual, between the couple, and even between parents and children. The couple's new relationship, whether a "together-relationship," or a "separate-relationship," is clearly based on choice rather than the force of circumstance, fear, default, or inadequacy.

THE SEPARATION STRUCTURE

The separating couple is asked to make a three-month commitment to explore themselves and the relationship. During this time both will see the counselor—optimally once a week. They are seen both individually and together. Sometimes one comes regularly and the other only as he or the therapist deems necessary.

During this time the couple is asked not to live in the same house, not to see a lawyer, and not to make any permanent financial, property, or child custody arrangements. Children remain in their own home with whichever parent is best able to care for them. Their lives are disrupted as little as possible. It is important that they maintain contact with such environmental supports as friends and school. As the couple communicates with each other while realistically assessing their needs, they resolve practical issues. Decisions are made out of the awareness of both partner's needs, not out of fear, guilt, or revenge.

Each partner agrees to be together only if, when, how, and as long as BOTH are comfortable. This choice rule applies also to parent-child contacts. Each is free to initiate contact; each is free to end contact when he wants to, for whatever reason. The couple may have sex together only if both want to.

At the point of making the commitment to the separation structure, the couple is encouraged to express feelings about outside affairs. Freedom to explore other relationships is encouraged on the theory that such exploration maximizes choice. If the couple decides to come together again, each knows it is because he is desired over and above others. In addition, a variety of social, emotional and sexual encounters gives each a more realistic view of himself interacting with others. These contacts serve to eliminate "If it weren't for you" games. They also cut through the "I was too young and inexperienced," "Nobody else would want me," and "I had to get married" types of excuses for discontented clinging.

During these three months, the couple learns to relate to each other in terms of needs, feelings, qualities of being, defenses and games. The process of seeing each other *only by choice* requires that each examine himself and the other often to decide whether or not to be together and when and how to reject the other. In this process of repeatedly accepting and rejecting, each has an extraordinary opportunity to learn to be honest with the other in communicating love, appreciation, and need as well as hurt, fear, and anger. Each may thus learn to take responsibility for gratifying his own needs.

Honesty comes more easily during this structured separation because the couple now has little to lose. In choosing to face the ultimate loss, risks are taken which would not ordinarily be taken for fear of losing. The knowledge that one can survive financially and emotionally apart from the other and that there are alternative ways of gratifying needs breeds courage. Fears and grievances are expressed; catastrophic expectations of hurt, loss and guilt are seldom realized. The way is cleared for the more positive feelings. One client stated after a few weeks of structured separation:

> We are talking about everything, and I feel much more free and she more loved. I also no longer feel that divorce would be such a cataclysm that I couldn't do anything that might bring it up. It feels more like a real option now, than like a threat. However, we are both trying now to see that it isn't necessary. In any case it beats lying, and suicidal fantasies, and continual frustration; and on the other hand independence no longer seems so frightening. It feels like a choice between positives now, instead of between a negative and an unknown.

A new relationship EVOLVES out of a multitude of honest choices. This is a "let it happen" rather than a "make it happen" approach. If the couple establishes a new "together-relationship," it will be strongest if each one, being maximally himself and doing and being that which allows him most growth and satisfaction, also meets the other's needs and allows him to grow and be satisfied. Love develops when each satisfies the majority of the other's basic interpersonal needs without sacrificing his own need-satisfaction.

The following case illustrates the separation structure:

Mr. and Mrs. W. had children three and five years of age. The W's had married because Mrs. W. was pregnant. She withdrew from school at age 17 and prematurely ended her adolescence. She resented her forced marriage, as well as her role as wife and mother. She wanted to return to school and to work. Mr. W. defined his manhood in terms of his ability to support his family. He held his wife to a high standard for housework, cooking, and child-care. He was demanding sexually, she was withholding.

The couple decided to divorce when Mr. W. discovered his wife's sexual involvement with a man six years her junior. Mr. W. then was uncomfortable about his decision and suggested they see a counselor. They subsequently agreed to delay their divorce for three months of separation counseling.

They decided to leave the children with Mr. W. in the family home. Their regular babysitter increased her time with them, thus providing consistent care while Mr. W. worked. The older child remained in school. Mrs. W. moved back to her parents' home, enrolled in night school and accepted a job. She did not ask for support money. She had managed the money for the family and knew there was not enough for two households. She visited the children three nights a week for their regular bedtime routine. They stayed with her at her parents' home every other weekend. The children were told the parents were having some problems being with each other now and were taking a vacation from each other for a while. Their difficulties were compared to difficulties the children had with their friends, where sometimes they didn't play together for a while.

Mrs. W's relationship with the young man ended a few weeks after her separation. She realized that she had involved herself with him more to express her resentment to her husband and to attempt to recapture her adolescence than because of the man's qualities. She dated heavily the first months of separation but found the men she now met were less interesting than her husband. She also found her sexual difficulties represented her own intra-psychic conflicts, and were not specific to her husband.

Mr. W., formerly highly moralistic and socially inhibited, did not begin to date until the second six weeks of separation. The fact that other women found him attractive boosted his self-esteem. Simultaneously he began to define his adequacy in terms other than money and sex. Mrs. W. found him more attractive as he was desired by others. She enjoyed his new ease in relating.

At first, Mr. and Mrs. W. saw very little of one another. He left the house when she came over and cursorily left the children with her on the weekend. Gradually, he stayed home more often when she put the children to bed. They began to talk over their differences and discuss their present experiences and feelings. Mr. W. tended to be possessive and jealous; Mrs. W. gradually saw how she taunted him with subtle threats of abandonment. Mr. W. saw how he tried to hold his wife with ever-increasing, unsatisfiable demands. Mrs. W. became aware of her use of passive-aggressive, manipulative behavior which frustrated and angered her husband. She became more direct in her refusal to accede to his demands; more willing to risk openly defining and satisfying her own needs. The couple explored new ways of solving problems through compromise. This couple also began to have fun together—a quality notably lacking in their marriage. They dated, danced, and played golf once a week while still dating others.

During the three month separation period, Mr. W's homemaking duties led him to be more realistic in his housework and child-care standards. Mrs. W. enjoyed her work, but found she did not enjoy school. With child-care voluntary, she found herself enjoying her children more and spending more time with them.

Sexual activities were resumed in the tenth week of separation. Intercourse was more satisfactory than it had been. Each was able to trust more and to be less controlling of self and other. With the diminution of frustration and anger, softness and warmth dominated their close time together. The sexual act became less important than the feeling between them.

The W's decided to reinstate their marriage after the 12th week of separation. Mrs. W. continued for a brief time in therapy to resolve her sexual conflicts.

SEPARATION COUNSELING

During the three-month time period, the separation counselor needs to attend to three major areas. These are: (1) the individuals' response to the separation; (2) the individuals' basic quality of being; and (3) the together-relationship:

RESPONSE TO SEPARATION: I have observed the following pattern among large numbers of separating people in singles groups and in clinical practice. People first experience a *shock reaction*. This is particularly obvious when the separation is sudden and unexpected. Most frequent expressions of this shock are denial and/or somatic disorder. Gastrointestinal disturbances, headaches, changes in eating patterns and upper respiratory infections are common. These are best attended to by a physician. The therapist's role is to use the symptom as meaningful content and help the client openly experience the pain rather than denying, avoiding or internalizing it.

The shock reaction is generally followed by an 8 to 12-week *affective cycle*. The first phase of this cycle is characterized by a four to six-week period of depression and withdrawal or by a similar period of euphoria and activity. During the following four to six-weeks, those who have depressed and withdrawn usually begin to feel more open and become more active. They seldom go as "high" as the group who were initially euphoric. Those who have at first been euphoric and active tend to withdraw and may become somewhat depressed. Again, the "low" tends to be less intense than that experienced by those initially depressed. This counter-reaction gradually shifts and stabilizes at an intermediate affective and activity level. It is on this base that the person can best either grow as a single individual or begin to establish a new dependency relationship.

One of the separation counselor's important functions is to help each client accept himself and the other as each experiences the various phases of this affective cycle. The period of withdrawal represents an unusual opportunity to introspect, to gain strength from one's own reserves, and to resist social pressure to "do something." The withdrawal period represents an opportunity to explore new directions that may be more meaningful than those followed before or during the marriage. This is a time when one may explore in fantasy plans to return to school, change employment, or even change careers. The excuse of "If it weren't for you and the marriage, I would have . . ." is, at least for the moment, not valid. This is a time to confront loneliness and to explore one's own resources. It is a time to become content in oneself as a separate individual. The danger here is that couples will prematurely reunite in order to avoid pain. The therapist's assurance that this is a time-limited and normal depressive reaction and his encouragement to "go with it" helps clients use this period creatively.

The period of euphoria and activity may be a natural response to the temporary freedom from conflict and the need to make an immediate final decision. People often experience genuine pleasure with their new freedom. However, euphoria may, especially if extreme, represent an avoidance of depression and grief. The individual, the partner, and the children are more accepting of this activity if it is understood as a separation reaction. The client is encouraged to use his interactions at this time to learn about himself. As he engages in other relationships he is better able to understand himself, the marriage, and its failure. Repressed anger may pour out during this period of activity. This is particularly true for people who have played "good guy" in the marriage and have "done everything to keep the marriage together." This may also be a time in which the individual puts all of his energies into work. He may be particularly creative at this time, exploring and investing energy in new areas of competence.

Ambivalence is inherent to separation and is a prominent factor in the affective cycle. That the people stayed together at all indicates the existence of some positive value to the relationship. Some needs are still being gratified. The effectiveness and extent to which each gratified the other's needs may be measured by the pain experienced on threat of loss. A great deal of negativity and anger also exists or the partners would not be separating. Most people find ambivalence difficult to sustain. It represents helplessness and loss of control. To cope with ambivalence requires the ability to tolerate nonstructure, frustration, conflict, inconsistency, and the simultaneous existence of opposites.

A very common way to cope with ambivalence is to focus on either the positive or negative ends of the affective and attitudinal spectrum. We find those who profess undying love and idealization of the relationship, despite a history of unhappiness and strife. More commonly, we find people who hate and malign the other and who refuse to recognize the good that was in the relationship. This polarization of attitude is often found among people who have blocked from awareness one or more feeling states. Emotions are used defensively. Thus, those who idealize often are afraid of their anger. Anger may be used to defend against tender feelings. It is often a defense against the pain of loss and/or fear. Both anger and love may be used to avoid sadness, feelings of helplessness and hopelessness, or the need to face oneself. When therapist and client focus on the missing feelings, a more realistic emotional balance is attained.

Polarization of attitude in addition to being a defense against ambivalence, may also be a symptom of decision-making difficulty. When one cannot easily order data in terms of relative importance, or when one has depended on external events or people to determine one's life-pattern, then there is a tendency to focus inappropriately on one aspect of a complex whole. The distorted view of the whole thus produced tends to make whatever decision one makes a necessity—a foregone conclusion.

Maintaining appropriate ambivalence puts parents in closer touch with their children. Children in a separating family generally maintain their mixed feelings. The problem of divided loyalties is minimized when parental attitudes and feelings remain balanced and realistic. Parents who can tolerate ambivalence are less prone to communicate feelings through their children or to force an emotional position on their children.

This 8 to 12-week affective cycle forms the basis for the three month time period found to be necessary for effective separation counseling. Both phases of this cycle represent adaptive reactions to the situation. Decisions made during this reactive period are often the result of such factors as relief that the pain of conflict is over, or are made out of fear of the unknown, shame, and sense of failure. After the period of reaction to the past relationship and the separation situation, and after the individuals have used this time to fully assess themselves and their ways of being together, they can then make decisions based on their present needs and value systems. Premature return to the marriage is avoided, as is premature and perhaps unnecessary separation on inappropriate "rebound" marriage.

The case of Mr. and Mrs. B. illustrates the importance of working through the affective cycle. It also indicates the value of focusing on the individual's quality of being.

Mrs. B., an aggressive social worker, came for help when her marriage was terminated by her husband, a shy engineer who had just finished school. He had discovered she had seduced his best friend. The couple was seen together once. Mr. B. refused to be involved in the structured separation process. Instead, he plunged into a relationship with an exotic dancer during the first week after rejecting his wife. Within a week after meeting, the dancer and her eight year old daughter moved in with him. They were later married but divorced after two years.

Mrs. B. was advised to remain in therapy for at least three months so that she might be guided through the affective cycle. She began the cycle with a severe depression and colitis. She decided to "go with" the depression and take a sick-leave from work. When she thus "gave in," the colitis disappeared. The content of her therapy sessions were first dominated by self-castigation, anger directed at her busand, jealousy, and fear that she would never find another man. She now found the man she had seduced repulsive. She alternately idealized and denigrated her husband. She tried desperately to get him back. Her tears were of rage and helplessness. They also were manipulative. Gradually she began to accept her husband's adamant refusal to reinstate their relationship or even to explore the dynamics which led to her inappropriate behavior. With this acceptance of reality, she began to experience genuine sadness and to mourn the loss of her marriage and her husband. She had previously repressed tears of sadness, considering such tears a sign of weakness.

She returned to work after two weeks and functioned reasonably well. She avoided contact with men; had little contact with women. She became interested in returning to school and the possibility of a new profession. She had worked during the marriage to support her husband. It appeared that her need to control her husband was now being directed toward the control of her own life.

During the fifth week after beginning counseling, she entered into a sexual relationship that was, like her marriage, characterized by manipulation and hostility on her part. This relationship was explored in terms of her needs and intra-psychic conflicts and its similarity to her marriage. The relationship lasted about three weeks.

She began to shift toward the active part of the affective cycle during this relationship. First, she bought new clothes. Second, she moved to an apartment closer to the school which she planned to attend. This was in a neighborhood in which she had always wanted to live. She began phoning some old friends, going to office parties, and dating a few men. Her need to control and manipulate was a major focus of counseling. Her fear of emotional freedom was an important factor underlying this behavior.

During this part of the cycle, she began to find ways to talk to her husband directly, rather than manipulatively. She met his girl-friend and recognized the futility of changing his attitude toward her. They then were able to talk about their feelings for each other in the present and explored ways to end the marriage on good terms. He gave her emotional support while she cried and together they mourned the loss of their marriage. This interaction represented a rare moment in which Mrs. B. was able to trust another person to take care of her when she was feeling vulnerable. Her inability to trust and to be comfortably dependent clearly surfaced as a major reason for the failure of this marriage. Mrs. B. was advised to continue therapy beyond the three month period to resolve her dependency and control conflicts. She was not willing to do this. She followed through on her plan to return to school. She deepened her friendship with a man in her new apartment building and after a year, married him. That marriage has remained intact a year. In choosing this husband, she attended particularly to his ability to stand up to her controlling qualities.

THE INDIVIDUAL'S BASIC QUALITY OF BEING: How the individual functions in general, aside from the specific separation situation, is an important area in separation counseling as in any therapeutic system. In separation counseling, emphasis is placed on the following factors: dependency and control needs and conflicts, the range of feelings available to the individual and how they are expressed, risk-taking behavior, ways of coping with loss, reactions to freedom, and value systems. Focus here is more on individual growth and development than on the relationship.

Dependency and control patterns and conflicts become quite clear when the person on whom one has depended and controlled—or has been controlled by—is gone. These patterns become increasingly apparent in the new tasks for which each partner is now responsible, the way in which each accepts responsibility for himself, and what each seeks in others to supplement or complement his own perceived inadequacies.

During these three months the counselor helps the individuals to perceive and accept dependency and control needs and to find growth-promoting ways to satisfy them. The value of an equal and interdependent relationship is stressed. Manipulative maneuvers to insure security and control are discouraged; honest communication of needs and the willingness to gratify needs is encouraged.

An inability to experience and express the full range of *feelings* may have been an important factor contributing to the marital crisis. Emotional limitations will affect subsequent relationships. This time of stress is extremely valuable for opening long-closed emotional channels. Separation involves the arousal of a complex set of emotions. Some positive feeling is there, whether it be love, the memory of love, liking, or need. Sadness or grief is a natural concomitant of loss. Anger is always present as a response to the hurt and frustration of basic needs that bring people to the point of separation. Anger is a common response to the problems that accompany adapting to new ways of living. Fear almost always accompanies risk, and risk is an essential ingredient of change. People often experience some sense of helplessness and hopelessness. Many individuals find separation especially difficult because they remain hopeful when such hope is not warranted. Feelings of guilt and shame are also generally present.

The effective separation counselor is aware of "missing" emotions. He helps individuals (1) perceive their lack, (2) understand how other feelings or thoughts are inappropriately substituted, and (3) develop an awareness of and willingness to in some way deal with those feelings heretofore repressed. Often such repression is accomplished by creating a fantasy image of oneself, the other, or the relationship. Such "defensive fantasies" do help the individual avoid certain feelings; they also prevent effective problem solving. In separate counseling, fantasy is replaced by the awareness of the reality of the situation. With this reality as a base, most problems and differences are easily resolved and the choice of leaving or maintaining the relationship is more easily made.

Risk-taking is inherent in the process of change that accompanies separation. The more risks one takes, the more opportunity for growth. This is a time for choice, change, and freedom. This is a time to "do your thing" honestly and openly: to "do nothing" during the depressed/withdrawn time; to engage the world in new ways during expansive times. This is a time when one can intensely experience every facet of existence.

Separation involves *role change*. Individuals change from marriage roles to single roles, perhaps from housewife to worker, from full-time parent to part-time parent, from accepted partner to rejected partner. A newly separated person must cope with the loss of old roles and "trained" reciprocal role-players. They must meet new role expectations and behavior.

Sometimes people who separate change their lives so extensively that they establish new roles and new role patterns. Or, they may maintain their former role patterns but find new people or situations to play the reciprocal role (i.e. a "helper" needs someone to "help"; a dependent person needs someone to depend on). In any event they must experience some disequilibrium while these patterns are in flux. The extent of distress experienced in making these role changes depends on the kinds of risk each takes and how gracefully and appropriately transitions are made.

Risk and change automatically involve *loss*. Each loss needs to be recognized as such and some consideration made of the meaning to the individual of the pattern and relationships lost, of his feelings about the loss, and how he goes about replacing the loss. Losses need to be mourned and thus made "finished business"* The process by which one deals with loss is fully as important as establishing new behaviors, attitudes, roles, feelings, or relationships to replace the old. How change is accomplished is as important as what change is made. Equally important is an awareness of reluctance to change and to risk. If one does not want to risk the unknown, he can gain much by learning to accept that to which he clings.

Separation makes new *freedom* suddenly available. Freedom can be frightening. Fear of freedom and its accompanying responsibility is found especially among individuals who need an external object for support, projection or control. Many couples separate in the belief that the other is restricting freedom to experience life fully. Others cling to a relationship to avoid this freedom. Awareness of each individual's ability to use freedom at this time is helpful in alleviating conflict clarifying dependency and control patterns, and the limitations each individual places on himself.

Value systems change over a period of years, but the changes are often not defined. Thus, for example, a couple may begin marriage with home and children agreed upon as a primary value. One partner may change and begin to place career or money above his family. Values placed on openness vs. secrecy, flexibility vs. rigidity, monogamy vs. sexual freedom, permissive vs. authoritarian child rearing often change for one and not the other. Or, it may be that before marriage, the couple did not believe that differences in these

---

*For a more complete discussion, see Chapter 6, "Understanding the Child of Di vorce," the section on *The Mourning Process*.

value dimensions were important. Making each individual's values explicit helps both understand the basis for some conflicts. It also helps individuals make decisions, take risks, and clarify life goals.

Mr. and Mrs. A. agreed to separation counseling after a stormy 17 year sado-masochistic marriage. Mrs. A., a depressed, dependent, inadequate woman clung desperately to her alcoholic husband. Mr. A. felt trapped and angry. He was uncomfortable with his children. He found them intrusive and unsatisfying. Yet he feared divorce would damage the children more than his continued presence in the home. He did not believe his wife could cope with the children alone.

Mr. A.'s work led to his transfer to a city two hours from their home after a year of marriage counseling in which neither could leave the other. They decided to take this opportunity to try structured separation. Both continued to be seen weekly. The children were seen once.

The father visited the children sporadically; they visited him twice. He found the limited, structured time with them more comfortable then the unstructured time at home. He became more giving to them of material goods, less hostile, and in general a better masculine model. They grew less fearful and more accepting of him. With his change, they began to wish for his return home and to feel guilty for their parents' separation. The children's guilt was dispelled as the counselor and the parents helped them see the marriage more realistically.

Mrs. A.'s depression began to lift after separation. She became more openly angry with her husband as she felt less frightened by his physical presence. She worked through her fears and anger with the counselor so her negative feelings did not interfere with the children's more positive attitudes toward their father. Mrs. A. gradually took more effective control over the children and also became more giving of her time and attention to them. She transferred some of her dependency needs to them, some to women friends, and some to the therapist.

It gradually became clear that she was better able to function when she was in control of her life. She became frightened and negativistic as soon as an adult made demands on her. Her children's demands were not so threatening. It also became clear that she was not so inadequate as she appeared to be.

Mrs. A. deepened her relationship with women friends. She dated a few times, but was too frightened of men to feel comfortable. Though she had resented her husband's drinking, she now began to drink and frequent bars. This behavior was dealt with in therapy in terms of the needs her husband's alcoholism had gratified. In part, his nightly visit to the bar allowed her to be alone a great deal. At the same time, she enjoyed his financial support and the protection, role definition and status of marriage. She had used the relationship to maintain her position as a child with a harsh father. She had clung to it to avoid the problems of adulthood. Separation meant she had to risk being responsible for her own decisions.

Mr. A. had used his bar activities to avoid being at home. With separation and his own apartment, his drinking decreased. He was not depressed after separation, but he was relatively withdrawn and quiet. His pre-separation affective level had been dominated by anger; he now experienced more warmth and softness. In the second month of separation, he became involved with his secretary. She was a strong woman who enjoyed drinking and was not cowed by his authoritarian manner. Her strength allowed him to gratify his dependency needs. His self-esteem rose as he found his values and his way of being acceptable to her.

The A.'s first contacts after separation were relatively frequent. They went out with friends who had not known of their separation. When alone, they were at odds with each other. Mr. A. continued to make sexual advances to which Mrs. A. reluctantly acceded. After the first month they saw each other only when he came for the children. Mrs. A. was now capable of openly rejecting him when she was uncomfortable in his presence. Mr. A. became less demanding. His self-worth became increasingly defined in terms of his own strength in equal interpersonal relationships, rather than in terms of his ability to dominate his family. They became less and less interested in each other as the three months came to an end.

This couple decided not to reinstate their marriage. A property settlement was made which insured the children's stay in the family home and psychotherapy for both children and mother. Alimony was arranged to be paid on a decreasing scale over a ten year period. This was intended to allow Mrs. A. to gain her strength, learn work-skills, and encourage self-sufficiency. It was deemed most advisable to discourage her use of helplessness to control others.

THE TOGETHER RELATIONSHIP: The separation counselor attends both to the way the couple interacts during joint sessions and to the number and the quality of contacts outside of the counselor's office. The counselor works with them as he would in any joint therapy situation. In addition, he remains aware of the separation process and the way in which each is coping with it. He shares his awareness with the couple so that they may understand and work with separation-related behaviors in proper context. The time-commitment structure gives the counselor as well as the couple the opportunity to work through situations which otherwise would very likely precipitate divorce (i.e., being open about sexual relationships with others).

In the course of the three months, some couples like Mr. and Mrs. W. continue to communicate, work through their differences, and learn more satisfactory patterns of mutual need gratification. By the end of the time, they choose to be together more often than they choose to be apart. They have proportionately more positive than negative interactions. These couples make a new together relationship. Other couples spend enough time together to explore their relationship and to understand each other, and yet their time together leaves them unfulfilled. They tend to choose to be apart more often than they are together. At the end of the three-month period they generally agree to finalize their separation. Some couples continue to be together more often than they are apart, but important conflicts remain unresolved. These couples may make a commitment to another period of structured separation; or they may structure a time-limited trial together-relationship. In the latter case, they are asked to make their own contract setting forth what each expects of the other and what each is willing to give to the other. Counseling continues until the couple is comfortable with a decision to come together or to part.

In a one-year follow-up of 18 couples who completed structured separation with counseling, six reinstated their marriage and were satisfied with the new relationship; 12 divorced. Of these twelve, only one couple needed legal help in making a property settlement. All but one of the couples have maintained good feelings toward each other, and all felt they have made the right choice. One extremely dependent, border-line psychotic man experienced some disorganization of function for several months after finalizing the separation. The other 23 separating individuals had gained equilibrium as single people by the end of the time they agreed to finalize their separation.

Summary

Structured separation with counseling offers couples in conflict a method by which they can use the separation crisis to maximize growth. Couples commit themselves to a three-month period during which they agree to certain basic guidelines: to live apart; not to make any binding legal, financial, or child-custody arrangements; to be together only by *choice*. Prime importance is placed on values of choice, risk, and honesty.

By focusing on both individuals' reaction to separation, their personality structures, and their evolving together relationship, a counselor's interventions help each partner through the various phases of the separation process.

At the end of the three-month period, people generally have a firm understanding of themselves and their relationship. The decision whether to finalize the separation or reinstitute the together-relationship tends to evolve out of the time and counseling structure.

REFERENCES

Parad, J.: *Crisis Intervention: Selected Readings.* New York, Family Services Association of America, 1965.

CHAPTER 8

TECHNIQUES OF GROUP MARITAL THERAPY

JOHN G. CULL *and* RICHARD E. HARDY

▲ ▲ ▲ ▲ ▲ ▲ ▲ ▲ ▲ ▲ ▲ ▲ ▲ ▲ ▲ ▲ ▲ ▲ ▲ ▲

▲ ▲ ▲ ▲ ▲ ▲ ▲ ▲ ▲ ▲ ▲ ▲ ▲ ▲ ▲ ▲ ▲ ▲ ▲ ▲

MARITAL ROLES IN GROUP COUNSELING

OFTEN IT IS DIFFICULT to discriminate between actual behavior and behavior which is related by a marriage partner. This period of counseling is difficult; the marriage counselor is interacting on a one-to-one basis or is occasionally seeing both marriage partners together. As a result of the defensiveness and the ego-protective nature of the individual client, quite often there is a great degree of uncertainty in the mind of the therapist as to the reality of the roles which are being reported to him and when it is evident that there is a reality base for some of the reports he receives from an antagonistic spouse, the question remains concerning the impact of this reported role, the substance of the role, and its prevalence. When a marriage starts deteriorating, it is quite natural for each partner to try to justify his position and to displace blame and responsibility for the deterioration of the marriage through recriminations and the imputing of negative roles on the other partner.

Group work is an ideal approach to be used in separating and understanding these diverse roles which are so basic in the marital interaction. As the therapist observes the individuals and their roles within the group, he can make a direct connection between the role an individual adopts in the group setting and the one he tends to play most often in the marital setting. In individual counseling, the client may appear somewhat passive, withdrawn, taciturn, and relate his reaction to others and his reaction to events in a philosophical manner. However, in group interactions, it is quite possible for him to change drastically and become the aggressor rather than the passive receptor in a relationship. The following types of behavior are deleterious to a marriage and may be observed in the marriage relationship. We will discuss them as they fall along a continuum from highly aggressive behavior through the acceptance seeker, the sympathy seeker, the confessor, the externalizer, the isolate, the dominator, and the antagonist. Many of these roles will not be exhibited in individual counseling with the marriage partner; however, the group therapist will see them emerge as the group begins to interact.

The Aggressive Individual

As mentioned above, an individual may appear somewhat passive in his relationship to others and his reaction to events may appear as if he is a passive receptor in a relationship. However, when observed in a group setting, it may become obvious that a drastic change has occurred and in reality he is a highly aggressive individual. As an aggressor, he may work many ways to exert his will. He may be oblivious or unconcerned about the feelings of others. He may override their concerns by deflating them, attempting to relegate them to lower status, either expressing disapproval or ignoring their feelings, their value system, or the acts in which they engage which are counter to his basic goals. He will appear to be highly goal-oriented regardless of the cost in achieving that goal and he will work toward the goal regardless of the hurt feelings, the damage to his interpersonal relationships. He works toward the goal which he perceives as the one bringing him most recognition. Under this set of circumstances, this individual will be most manipulative in that he will show the highest degree of Machiavellianism in the group. He will be somewhat jealous of individuals who gain more recognition than he, and he will be sympathetic toward the individual whom he outshines most readily. Yet this individual may see himself as a somewhat passive person and have little or no understanding of the obvious sources of marital discord.

The Acceptance Seeker

Related to the individual who has a high degree of need to accomplish the goals he perceives as important and who accomplishes them through aggressive-type behavior is the individual whose concern is not the accomplishment of the goals but whose goal is to receive acceptance by the group or the person who feels the need for recognition within the group. This is an individual who is quite insecure and tends to need almost continual positive reinforcement as to his self-adequacy and his value to the group or to the marriage partner. This type of individual demonstrates his needs in the group in many ways. Generally, he will not be as oriented toward the goal which is perceived by the group as the group goal as will be the aggressive-type individual. But he will work toward the goal if he feels it will bring a great deal of recognition. Much of his overt behavior upon examination will be seen to be self-serving and self-gratifying behavior rather than goal-oriented behavior. It has been our experience in group work with marriage partners that this type of individual has many more needs than the aggressive-type individual. If the individual who is seeking the recognition to the exclusion of everything else has a spouse who attempts to meet these needs, quite often the needs are so great the spouse loses the impact she once had to fulfill his needs; therefore, he looks elsewhere for the recognition which is so essential to his personality integration. He responds to her as being unconcerned about him, as not really understanding his motivations, and may give the impression that the spouse is somewhat self-centered and uncooperative in the marriage pact. In the group situation, the individual demonstrates his need for recognition by behavior and mannerisms both verbal and nonverbal which call attention to himself. He quite often will boast; he will feel the need to relate personal experiences; he will relate his accomplishments and achievements; perhaps he may relate them in a thinly veiled manner under the guise of using them as an example to make a point in some other area; however, he feels compelled to bring forth his accomplishments, his values, his attributes to the group and to hold them out for group approval. His most painful moments in the group will be when he perceives he has been devalued by other members in the group and placed in an inferior position or when he feels he is demonstrating behavior which is characterized by the group as inadequacy.

The Sympathy Seeker

On a continuum down from the aggressive-type individual on to the individual who is seeking recognition from the group, the next type of personality may be characterized as the sympathy seeker. This individual attempts to elicit responses of sympathy from the group thereby obviating any pressures for him to achieve either within the group or without the group. As he depreciates himself and relegates himself to a lower inferior position, he gets the sympathy of the group and at the same time is absolved of responsibility within the group. This provides him a haven of irresponsibility. He is able to go his own way; he can follow the group or he can elect to remain aloof from the group all with the approval of the group as a result of his being in a position to receive sympathy from the group. As the group becomes more demanding and insistent on his contributing, he will reinforce his protestations of inferiority or illness, of devaluation or of a generalized inadequacy. He will attempt to reinforce the group's feelings of sympathy for him in order to free himself from intanglements of the group. If he is unsuccessful in his attempts to get sympathy from the group, he will attempt to split the group into smaller units and will seek statements of sympathy from the smaller subgroups. The value of the group interaction is to denote how an individual who is a sympathy seeker in the group setting but when seen in the marriage relationship and on an individual counseling basis may come through as a relatively independent sort of person who expresses feelings of adequacy and concern for the marriage relationship. The group setting will highlight change when his behavior is observed and the pressures of the group are exerted.

The Confessor

The next type of behavior which is brought out in a group is the confessing behavior. This is behavior that is characterized by rather superficial confessing. As the individual sees that the demands are getting greater to reveal himself and as he sees that his responsibility will have to be fulfilled if he is to maintain membership in the group, quite often he starts confessing in a very superficial manner to the group. Generally, these confessions are characterized by large quantity with a very low quality. He feels that the more he confesses, the more he absolves himself of responsibility for honest group interaction. He confesses to his feelings which are somewhat insignificant in a very sober, concerned fashion. He professes to have immediate insight as a result of the group sessions. When an individual starts to criticize him, this confessing-type individual immediately stifles the criticism or stifles the comments by agreeing with the critic and going even further in confessing these feelings or attributes and feelings and attributes related to these on and on *ad nauseam*.

In a marriage, confessing-type behavior is a very effective defense. It is quite frustrating when a marriage partner tries to communicate and is thwarted by the other marriage partner's superficial self-confessing behavior. Communication in this instance is effectively blocked when one marriage partner evades a confrontation with the other marriage partner by this superficial type of confessing behavior. When this type of behavior is exhibited, it is quite difficult to get to the core of the problem in individual counseling since the confessor is verbalizing a great deal of concern, flexibility, and willingness to cooperate when in fact his behavior is aimed more at stifling communication and blocking effective understanding within the marriage relationship. By adopting this defensive behavior, he is not required to engage in a confrontation with the other marriage partner. He is able to maintain interaction on a relatively superficial level.

The Externalizer

Another type of behavior which is exhibited in groups can be characterized by the term "externalization." The externalizer is an individual who becomes uncomfortable in the interaction and the "give and take" which is occurring in the group or which occurs in close interpersonal relationships, he tends to focus on problems that are external to the group or external to the relationship. As the group starts to focus on the individual or as the group gets too close to the individual, he starts externalizing in order to shift the brunt of an attack or the brunt of an inquisition from him on to some external object. Quite often this can be a very effective maneuver; however, again, it is one which is highly frustrating to an individual who is seriously trying to resolve conflicts. An effective externalizer is able to communicate his values, his impressions, his attitudes and beliefs very effectively without referring to himself. He does this through interjecting or projecting his attitudes into the attitudes of groups external to the interaction he is currently engaged in. Consequently, he is able to communicate a point of view which he holds without allowing others to adequately communicate their points of view.

The Isolate

The next type of behavior which is observed in the group setting and has a direct referent back to marital interactions is the isolate. This is the individual who decides to insulate himself from the interaction of the group. He very definitely elects not to interact with the group and decides to disallow the group now interacting with him. He quite often will make a very studied effort to inform the group of his nonchalence, of his decision to be noninvolved. He does this quite often by engaging in stratagems which are distracting to the group but which give no indication of his interest or willingness to contribute to the group. He may attract the attention of one or two other members of the group and start to play with them. He may become very animated in doodling. He may develop little games which he plays with himself such as folding paper, making airplanes, drawing pictures of the room. When confronted, his general response is, "I'm paying attention," "I'm listening," "I'm participating," "I just engage in these little activities to heighten my sensitivity to what's going on." This individual generally will not allow himself to be drawn into the interaction within the group. He will stay outside the mainstream of activity and will attempt to communicate his intentions to stay outside the mainstream of activity through nonverbal behavior. His verbal behavior will be one of conciliation and concern.

The Dominator

The next type of behavior on the continuum from highly goal-oriented to highly negativistic will be the individual who tries to dominate one or more individuals in the group or tries to dominate the entire group. His drives toward domination are an effort to convince others of his authority and of his superiority. His interests are not as goal-oriented as the aggressive-type individual who sacrifices others' feelings and his own interpersonal relationship with others in an effort to accomplish a group goal; however, the dominating-type individual is concerned with exerting influence over others not for the goal which can be achieved but just for the sake of dominance. If there is a highly aggressive individual in the group and a dominating individual in the group, the more maladaptive type of behavior will be exhibited by the dominating individual for he will find the need to express his adequacy by wooing group members away from the goal-oriented aggressive-type individual whose drives are to move the group toward a goal. The dominator will achieve his purpose if he subverts the actions or intents of the aggressive individual. The dominating individual is concerned with achieving a status of respect. He may do this through many types of behavior such as being punitive and using the threat of punitive behavior to tower a weaker member. He may use flattery to woo a member. He may use the power of suggestion and persuasion or he may just attempt to verbally and socially overpower the other individuals to force them into submission. In a marriage relationship, this type individual most often has to have a wife who is somewhat passive and one who does not have a high level of need for individuality and expressions of self-adequacy through the approval of their spouse.

The Antagonist

The next and last type of behavior to be discussed is the antagonist. This is the individual who strives for self-adequacy and recognition through the negativistic behavior and values he adopts. He is somewhat arbitrary and capricious in his value judgments. The underlying constant of his judgments is the contrariness of his position. He seems to be at odds with the mainstream of opinion, values, or actions within the group interaction. His negativism can be quite harsh and sharp. He apparently is unconcerned about the feelings of others in the group. The most important thing to him is to exhibit his individuality by disagreeing with the group consensus. He is stubbornly resistent to coercion or persuasion. He will go so far as to disrupt the flow of the work of the group by attempting to change directions, change the topic of concern, alter the goal which the group is working toward, or try to redefine the ground rules which were established in the group. This antagonist takes a negative view of life and is antagonistic to almost all of the members in the group. He is argumentative and can be quite bombastic when thwarted.

Individual and Group Approaches

There is an exercise in group behavior which requires working toward the solution of a problem concerned with being marooned on the moon. The problem requires individuals to react by rank ordering a number of various types of equipment which they would choose to have with them if they were so marooned. The exercise which has been checked by space experts at the National Space and Aeronautics Administration is first completed by individuals and later by a group of six to eight persons working together. The usual result of the exercise is that group behavior is demonstrated over and over again to be more effective in getting at correct solutions to problems than has individual effort alone. In some few cases the individual's decision may be more effective than that of the group, but in most cases the group decision is more clearly correct than the individual one.

The purpose of the exercise is to demonstrate the effectiveness of group interaction in problem solving. Just as the exercise does demonstrate the effectiveness of increased interaction among individuals in problem solving, so does group marital counseling achieve much more in many cases than does the basic interaction between the client and therapist. While much can be accomplished by individual sessions with the client, it is our feeling that supplemental group sessions can bring about enormous strides in understanding and adjustment.

In marital counseling, it is essential to see the clients in an individual one-to-one situation. It is equally important to see spouses together; however, we feel that it is of utmost importance for effective marriage counseling to supplement individual counseling with group techniques, for it is through group techniques that much of the behavior which can remain enigmatic in individual counseling is delineated and exemplified by pressures and interactions of the group. Much of the behavior which has constituted irritant factors of the marriage pact are elicited in the group situation and comes to surface there.

This behavior which is apparent in the group setting can be observed by the therapist, and in the individual sessions which follow, this observed behavior can be related to the individual and interpreted for him to review and evaluate and react to. Without benefit of the group, marital counseling is much slower and a much longer process. Many times, marriage will continue to deteriorate at a rate faster than that at which the therapist is able to diagnose and treat the irritants precipitating the deterioration.

Selection of Group Participants

In group marital counseling one generally has a decision to make concerning whether he wants to have in his group only husbands, only wives or mix the group. He also needs to make a decision whether husbands and wives will be in the same group. When husband and wife are in the same group, other members of the group can help them explore in considerable detail their problem areas. When husbands or wives are in groups made up of exclusively all males or all females the group leader will experience some difficulty in keeping the session from turning into a type of complaint session about the opposite sex. When husbands and wives are in groups separately from one another group members have been shown to be very eager to help the individual to explore his marital situation and understand it more fully. The best combination seems to be one in which both husband and wife are in the same group or husband or wife are in mixed groups of males and females. Heterogeneity has a great effect upon the effectiveness in group interaction and problem solving. Diversity brings with it certain breadth of experience and increases the strength of the group to solve both individual problems and group problems. Persons from all walks of life can be mixed in a heterogenious marital group counseling situation. This same opinion would extend to persons of various ages and socioeconomic backgrounds.

RELATIONSHIPS NECESSARY FOR EFFECTIVE
GROUP INTERACTION

Some of the necessary ingredients for effective group problem exploration include acceptance of others, awareness, self-acceptance of individuals in the group, and problem centering approaches to behavior. When these conditions exist a high "trust" level has been achieved. People are free to be themselves when a level of trust has been established in the group. When the "trust" level has not been established or is low, group members tend to be manipulative, to hold back information about themselves, and to be defensive. When individuals within the group trust one another, defensiveness is reduced, information flow is multiplied, and the strategies of manipulation are dissipated.

The group leader must create in members a feeling of freedom. They can be most valuable as group members to others in groups and themselves when they are free and able to be themselves.

Modeling Behavior

It is the responsibility of the group leader to model the types of behavior which he would like to see exhibited by the various members of the group. The group facilitator or leader should not be overbearing or dominating as a leader but should move the group toward understanding of problems through various behaviors which he not only demonstrates but models. The group leader should be an individual who is friendly, warm, and accepting. He should be a person who works with others and does not practice techniques upon them. The word "with" suggests that the procedure taking place is a relationship and not a technique oriented process. The atmosphere within the group should be productive of or conducive to good mental and social-psychological health. The goal of all group work is that of the obtainment of good mental health.

Every member of the group should be accorded enough consideration and respect by the group in order that he has at least a modicum of self-esteem. The individual must be willing and able to accept himself within a group setting. He must feel that he has the respect of others and that he is a person of worth. The group environment should facilitate the development and maintenance of self-esteem.

Members of the group should show considerable acceptance of

others and their attitudes regardless of whether or not group members agree with the attitudes or ideas which are being expressed. In other words, group members do not have to agree with the ideas in order to accept them as legitimate personal feelings of the individual expressing them. At times the needs of individuals in the group for self-esteem may interfere with their accepting and respecting others. It has been shown many times that we may want to feel superior to others and we do this by bolstering ourselves. When this is the case, often the person involved does not have enough respect for himself; therefore, he cannot respect others. Listening to another is the simplest and one of the most basic ways through which we can show respect for him.

Group members need to show understanding of others' feelings and the group leader should demonstrate that he understands how others feel and wishes to get to know them better. If the group leader uses psychological terminology glibly, he may "turn off" the group. He should not attempt to demonstrate understanding through such use of professional jargon, but he should demonstrate that he has what has been called accurate empathy in reference to the individual. He can put himself in the other's place and understand feelings as the other person experiences them.

All members of the group must demonstrate some degree of confidence in the other persons in the group. There must be recognition of the rights and privileges and freedoms to action of others. The group must be characterized by sincerity, integrity, openness, and honesty if it is to achieve its goals. These characteristics help eliminate the threat and help to create an enviroment in which the individual can develop to his fullest potential by exploring all aspects of his particular marital problem. The group leader should give his attention, respect, understanding, and interest to those within the group who are attempting to work toward a solution of their problems and help others in doing likewise.

Artificiality must be avoided on the part of the group leader at all costs. There is no real alternative to genuineness in the group counseling process.

The group leader must demonstrate the types of behavior which participants in the group need to exhibit if problem solving is to take place. There must be a certain amount of risk taking, in other words, individuals in the group must go beyond what is known to be factual in order to explore their behavior. Persons must be willing to do more than play it safe. If for instance, within a session an individual becomes angry or anxious, these behaviors can make him appear foolish; but these may be necessary behaviors and necessary risks to take in order for him to achieve success in problem solving. There must be substantial support for others as members attempt to reach goals that are important. Persons can say in various ways that they may not be sure what an individual is aiming toward or proposing, but they support the efforts being made to get something moving or to make others understand a particular problem.

There should be a demonstration that persons are free and able to be open about their feelings and thoughts, and there should be a problem centering or focusing on problems faced by a group rather than on control or method. Problem centering is based upon the assumption that the group can accomplish much more when individuals in groups learn how to solve problems rather than by the leader having to employ certain technique patterns in order to achieve goals. Group members should clearly recognize the feelings of others and how one's feelings are interinfluencing the behavior of others.

Another characteristic which is most important in achieving the level of problem solving ability necessary for success is that of the individual feeling that he can accept his own emotions without denying them or giving rationalizations or apologies. Such acceptance can be evidenced by such statements, "I am disgusted or bored with myself because I feel ineffective."

Problems Which May Surface During Group Marital Counseling

There is no end to the types of human situations which may come to light during marital counseling. Group marital counseling just as individual counseling and other group counseling covers the whole realm of human life and experience. Of course, there are sex problems which include frigidity, sterility, impotence and others. There are the problems of children, there are the problems of incongruencies in expectations, of differences in opinion concerning careers, there is the problem of extramarital relationships, of changing life styles in a rapidly moving society, of parents and in-laws and their influence in the marriage. There are identification problems, problems of personal values, the different meanings of love and substitutes for it which are meaningful to some people and not meaningful to others, the expression and management of feelings, the handling of various financial crises and many others.

The counselor concerned with group marital counseling must be a mature individual who is able to facilitate human learning through the demonstration of the behaviors described earlier. He must know group interactions well and thoroughly understand human behavior.

GROUND RULES FOR GROUP MARITAL SESSIONS

Human interaction includes two major properties: (1) content and (2) process. Content has to do with the subject matter with which the group is concerned. Process has to do with the actual procedure of what is happening between and to group members while the group is working. The group leader must be sensitive to the group process in order to help the group in diagnosing special problems so that these can be dealt with soon and effectively.

One of the important concepts in group interaction is that everyone who is in the group belongs there because he simply is there. Gendlin (1968) has indicated that this concept is one of the most important ones in effecting successful group behavior. If an individual gets angry with another person, this behavior does not change his belonging in the group. If a person reads himself out of a group, it does not change his belonging in it. If he gives up on himself, the group does not give up on him.

According to Gendlin, each person determines what is true for him by what is in him. Whatever he feels makes sense in himself and whatever way he wishes to live inside himself is determined by what is in him as an individual. Most people live mostly inside themselves. No one knows more about how a person really is than the person himself. The group leader should remember that he should force no one to be more honest than he wants to be just at the moment he is speaking. We should listen for the person inside the individual who is living and feeling. This person may not be totally exposed to us at any given time although he may wish to be exposed.

The group leader is always responsible for protecting the belong-ingness of every member to group and also their right to be heard. He is also responsible for the confidential aspect of the group dis-closures, which means that no one will repeat anything which has been said outside of the group unless it concerns only himself.

Everyone should participate in the group. One indication of in-volvement is verbal participation. The group leader should look for differences in terms of who are the high and low participators. What are the shifts in participation? How are the persons who are not participating being treated by the others? What subgroups are there? Who keeps the group moving? Which of the groups are high in terms of influence? Are there autocrats and peacemakers? Are there members getting attention by their apparent lack of involvement in the group? Who attempts to include everyone in group discussion decision making? In other words, what are the styles of influence? Is the group drifting from topic to topic? Is this a defensive type of behavior? Do they attempt to become overly organized at the expense of losing effectiveness in problem solving? Are there persons outside of the group?

Is the group avoiding certain topics and setting certain norms for behavior? Is religion or sex, for instance, avoided as a topic? Are the group members being overly nice to each other? Are they agree-ing too soon? In short are they avoiding facing individual and group problems?

One of the helpful techniques which can be used in group marital counseling is that of spontaneous role playing. This can be done by husband and wife sitting in the center of the group and playing out a particular problematic situation. The group members can then react to various aspects of the role playing and make suggestions in order that the individuals may develop fuller understanding of the prob-lem area. It may also be useful to have a surrogate wife or husband role play with an actual husband or wife.

Role reversal is another technique in which individuals reverse their roles and then role play actual situations. This technique can be most interesting in that the husband plays the wife's part and wife plays the husband's part. It is sometimes easy to bring about understanding through the use of this technique. Persons can relive past events or project future occurrences through role playing.

Another technique which is useful is that of repeating the client's key words or statements. This is particularly useful in terms of what has been called free association. In other words, that process of using clues or cues to help the client give meaningful information about himself and his problems.

The group leader should keep in mind that persons who live many psychosomatic complaints may be disguising personal problems and conflicts. He should also remember that the individual group member who offers any complaints about his spouse may be covering his own personal anxieties and inadequacies.

TIME PERIODS AND TYPES OF SESSIONS

The purpose of this chapter has been to describe group marital counseling. Generally, sessions may last for three to four hours and may be on-going, meeting eight to ten or more times. This varies from the individual counseling sessions which usually last from 50 to 60 minutes.

Much of the material given in this chapter concerns the facilitating of groups rather than the actual leading of them as a group therapist. It is felt by the authors that selected encounter group concepts can be of substantial benefit in various types of marital counseling.

Of course, it may be that group members will wish to engage in a type of marathon encounter in which they may continue their group activities for 20 to 24 hours. These sessions can later be followed by shorter two to three-hour sessions, follow-up groups for those who are interested. Group leaders should not become discouraged if some of their group members do not choose to return to later group meetings. People vary enormously in their abilities to withstand various types of stress and many people feel a good deal of insecurity and stress during group counseling work even though substantial efforts have been made to establish an atmosphere of warmth and trust. Some people are able to gain a great deal in a short period of time and for these persons, individual counseling may be more in accordance with their needs than group experiences.

The group counselor, leader, or facilitator—whichever name is chosen—must keep in mind that the purpose of the session is whatever goal the group decides upon. At times a group session may provide real service in terms of being informational in nature. One of the basic problems related to problems in marriage is the preparation for simply living with another person.

At times the counselor will find it necessary to assume the role of information giver and tutor in individual sessions and in group sessions members find it necessary to be informational in order to achieve basic goals which have been established. Group members can greatly help individuals in the group by exploring the needs of each person. In many cases unmet needs exist due to the fact that these needs are not understood by the spouse and often the person himself.

REFERENCE

Gendlin, E.T. and Beebe, J.: Experimental groups: Instructions for groups. In G.M. Gazda (Ed.): *Innovations to Group Psychotherapy*. Springfield, Ill., Charles C Thomas, pp. 190-206, 1968.

CHAPTER 9

MULTIPLE IMPACT THERAPY WITH FAMILIES: CURRENT PRACTICAL APPLICATIONS

ALBERTO C. SERRANO

BRIEF BACKGROUND OF THE METHOD

THIS CHAPTER will describe current applications of a family-centered treatment approach that was developed as Multiple Impact Therapy (McGregor, R. et al., 1964) at the University of Texas Medical Branch in Galveston, Texas. The MIT project, which studied 55 families of disturbed adolescents over a four-year period (1958-62), involved the use of a brief intensive treatment technique in which an orthopsychiatric team met with the family of an emotionally disturbed adolescent during two consecutive days, and included team family sessions, individual and group interviews with various combinations of team and family members. Its purpose was to study the brief therapy approach departing from the usual once a week format and attempted to use the cumulative impact and convergence of mental health professionals and family members meeting within a two-day period to enhance natural healing processes. We had earlier observed that families threatened with serious emotional and/or behavioral disturbance in a child often traveled long distances to the University of Texas Medical Branch in Galveston to consult the Youth Development Project, an outpatient psychiatric clinic for adolescents. We found, as did Gerald Caplan (1956), that the crisis not only facilitated the engagement of the family in seeking help but also opened the way to self-rehabilitating family processes with brief therapeutic intervention. Most of the techniques used in the MIT project had been reported by other group and family therapists separately (Peck, 1953; Johnson, 1953; Whitaker et al., 1949; Ackerman, 1958). The design included the use of multiple therapists in individual and group situations with the family members, often inviting relevant community representatives as conveners.

Follow-up studies that were routine at six and eighteen months indicate that the treatment results were comparable to more intensive long-term therapies. In forty-three of the fifty-five cases treated during the first two years of the project family self-rehabilitative processes remained effectively mobilized. In seven families the presenting problem was unchanged or worse. The impact of the technique was indicated by the fact that twenty-eight of the cases had continued toward self-rehabilitation after only the minimal procedure. Fifteen cases required more attention and led to longer term team-family centered work. This was particularly needed in cases of extreme psychopathology. This led us to develop more flexible applications of the basic design after the project was completed. Encouraging results were obtained with psychotic or near psychotic cases where the procedure was repeated every four to six weeks through the first year. We also found that the intervention at the time of intense crises with a stable and functional family responded favorably with one day or even half-day intake procedure resembling the first day of MIT followed by brief follow-up visits.

The Family Therapy Program in San Antonio

For the past several years, I have been in San Antonio, Texas as director of a private nonprofit out patient mental health clinic for children, adolescents and their families. The Community Guidance Center of Bexar County is affiliated with the University of Texas Medical School at San Antonio and serves a city-county of close to one million population that includes about 51 percent Mexican-Americans, 42 percent Anglos and 7 percent Blacks. The Center has a community mental health orientation and uses an ecological social systems approach to the understanding and the treatment of emotional, behavioral and learning disorders (Auerswald, 1972). Service and training run close together. The program underlines the importance of the family and of other significant social systems such as school, in the evaluation and treatment. All cases are assessed on a family centered basis with emphasis placed on short-term therapies including family and group treatment modalities. Those cases needing residential or day care treatment are referred to the San Antonio Children's Center, a psychiatric nonprofit mental health agency to which we are closely related through sharing staff and joint affiliation with the University of Texas Medical School at San Antonio. It also has a family centered philosophy. Let us examine now our population served and the manner in which the original MIT techniques have been adapted.

The Referral Network

In our program most referrals arise from schools, family and friends, medical practitioners, and social agencies. They represent all socio-economic and ethnic groups in close proportion to the Bexar County population. We find it essential to "think family" while working with other social systems notably schools, health and social agencies, churches and neighborhood centers. Caregivers of those systems are of crucial value as conveners of troubled families to get help from our staff. We often invite those community representatives for diagnostic work, planning, treatment, follow-up and further care. The use of an ecological approach involving other systems around the troubled family facilitates a more clear dynamic understanding of what appears pathological while concurrently assessing existing strengths and evoking self-rehabilitative processes. Including other systems in our work also teaches the families to negotiate with them more effectively and to attempt to change dysfunctional systems.

Priming a case at the referral level is of great importance. For example: how a principal of a school presents his referral to us to the family is often more important than what we say or do at the time of initial contact. Thus personally knowing the sources of referral, having shared respect and understanding for our different yet overlapping professional tasks greatly facilitates a relevant referral, with a family more willing to engage in therapeutic work, less prone to feel rejected or coerced by the referring agent. The family then will view our intervention as assistance to them rather than us as persecution or judgment.

The Initial Contact

Typically an intake worker who is a mental health paraprofessional is the first person to respond to the initial telephone call or the walk-in visit. The worker takes the initial referral data, explains the services available through the center and explains the need to meet with all family members—typically all those living at home and frequently other significant relatives. Considerable effort is applied to invite fathers who often receive a personal call to explain the significance of their presence. We suggest this be done by a male staff member preferably and of the same ethnic group. The father is invited to attend at least the initial evaluation session. Very often a reputedly uncooperative father comes willing to participate as a new authority is being defined for his role. The intake worker also may discuss the possible inclusion of a referring source as convener. A developmental questionnaire and forms for reports from the family physician and from the school are mailed to obtain further collateral information. That we have a charge on a sliding fee scale according to income is also brought up although the actual fee is set later.

Preparation for Evaluation

If the problem is an emergency or a crisis, the family may be seen on the same day or so without waiting for reports. Most cases however, are regularly scheduled and are seen within one to four weeks depending on the volume of service at the time and will come prepared to stay from two to three hours of initial evaluation.

The team to work with a particular family is assigned by preferably taking under consideration several factors: nature and severity of symptoms, sex, age, racial, cultural and religious background for a best possible match with staff and trainees. We have to take under consideration that a team may include child psychiatrists, psychologists, social workers, educational specialists, mental health paraprofessionals, medical students, child psychiatry fellows, psychiatry, psychology and pediatric residents, social work students, pastoral counseling and mental health worker trainees.

In making an ideal assignment it is very useful to match the family with a team ready to "speak the language" of the family. The use of paraprofessionals facilitates the engagement of the family while professionals provide a specific clinical competence to the diagnostic process. Considerable effort is required to reconfirm appointments with clients and to notify referral sources of these in order to minimize the non-shows and cancellations.

The Team

One or two staff members of different disciplines are typically included along with one or two trainees and when available the family convener. They review the existing material for about 15 minutes and discuss possible hypotheses and strategies, including tentative plans as to which team member will go with what division of the family when the separate sessions start. The senior member of the team most frequently will lead the group and act as "live supervisor." Those new to the method are encouraged to be active, for the ideal multiple therapy situation calls for active participation rather than for passive observation. Thus the ideal multiple therapy situation presents a smooth collaboration between the team members and provides a model for identification for the family members who often then will experience that it is possible for adults to communicate openly and respectfully. Excessive politeness on one hand and competitiveness on the other tend to interfere with the efficiency of the team intervention and greatly reduces its impact as a diagnostic and therapeutic agent. The proper climate is fostered by the senior therapist in the team who demonstrates by example the benefits of a team collaborating as an open system. Those who criticize the use of multiple therapy underline the difficulties of teaming up professionals. We have found that merely grouping a team, as an administrative decision, is often ineffective or disastrous or may end as a polite "low key" treatment intervention. Self-selection and the opportunity to openly discuss the development of the relationship with each other along with supervision and consultation is in our experience most effective in facilitating a climate of openness and growth. As the co-therapist relationship grows, they become more sensitive and responsive to the families.

There are two major functions that explain and justify the use of more than one therapist—one deals with specific treatment advantages and the other concerns the training of and consulting with psychotherapists. The complexities of treating more than one individual, as it is in the treatment of couples, families and groups make it extremely difficult and taxing for a single therapist to take on. The understanding and management of the multiple transferential problems is rather complex if at all accessible to one therapist's awareness. The co-therapy situation provides a "stereoscopic view" of the family and lends opportunity to the treatment twosome for a division of labor in which they may involve themselves at different levels, such as in a tennis match, where one plays in front while the other covers the back, enjoying enough flexibility so that they can alternate in their roles. The co-therapists also monitor each other and in so doing provide a growth model for themselves and for the group under treatment. Furthermore, the co-therapy model more effectively deals with the multiple transference problems encountered in treating families. It is also of special value for children and adolescents to witness adults who are able to deal openly and honestly with their agreements and disagreements and who promote a climate of respect and comradeship. As Whitaker and Napier said, the co-therapist "acts as a triangulating agent between the other therapist and the family" (1972). Also, since it can be a problem when the trainee tries to imitate and depend too much on his teacher's style and philosophy, we find it very important that trainees get a chance to work in co-therapy with different therapists, to experience other styles and learn about how senior therapists deal with feelings, beyond knowing of their intellectual abilities and technical skills.

Initial Team-Family Session

After a brief social phase of welcome and introductions (at which time permission may be requested for one way mirror observation or videotaping), the family is invited to describe in their own words what they see as their problem. An effort is made soon to give each member an opportunity to give his perspective of the situation.

It is frequent that at the initial team-family conference the family reports some degree of improvement since the referral contact and voices concern over the need for further evaluation. This is typical resistance aimed at blocking further study by the team. Other families are critical and uncomfortable about open discussion of problems in front of the children. We recognize their discomfort and assure them that observation of their patterns of communications is an essential part of the team's work and that they will have an opportunity to discuss more private matters in separate sessions. After an initial reluctance most families open up and start defining problem areas. Participating siblings and significant members of the extended family often reveal crucial material. Discrepancies, incongruencies or new historical data soon bring new light into the referring problem. Little effort is made at this point to extend the focus of intervention beyond the family's level of readiness to engage with the team in the helping process. Since the family typically came because one of their children presents behavioral, emotional and/or learning difficulties, they may want help just for that. Side taking, confrontation and interpretations are reserved for later in most cases. Respect for the gradual unfolding of historical material as the result of the growing process of team-family interaction in place of attempts to obtain a formal chronological history is also essential. It is our experience that low middle-class families expect us to be more direct, supportive, active and goal oriented than upper middle-class families, regardless of ethnic background. As other problem areas start emerging before the team, their intervention should reflect respect, concern, openness, curiosity, and some humor but never at the family's expense. Team members become mediators, go-betweens and help bridge communication between family members. This is demonstrated as team members check with each other and share impressions and feelings. This is particularly useful when a community representative is present as convener who has the trust of the family from earlier contacts. The initial team-family session generally lasts about 45 minutes to one hour by which time problem areas are more clearly defined and tension is sufficiently mobilized to facilitate considerable catharsis in the separate and individual sessions.

Separate Sessions

We regularly see the referred patient in an individual interview that later may be scheduled for further psychiatric, psychological or psychoeducational evaluation. Most often this interview is conducted by psychiatric or psychology staff for the purpose of formal diagnostic documentation. Interviews with parents, siblings and other separate conferences or any other boundary consideration are typically held according to family structure and the team's impressions. Often it is useful to see siblings together before seeing the nominal patient in a separate interview. We try to convey the attitude that while we deal initially with the symptoms presented by one family member, we are also concerned with the family structure and functioning as a whole, just as we are concerned with each individual member's functioning and feelings. We believe that to understand the family as a whole and its interpersonal transactions that include dyads, triads, and coalitions, we should not overlook the significance of the individual. Furthermore, it is essential to perceive the family in its ecological social context.

Separate conferences are run concurrently and for about 30 to 45 minutes. It is possible for an interviewer to leave a session to join another when there is something to be checked out or shared. The overlapping interview is an important contribution of the original MIT design and offers an unusual opportunity for developing more open communication within the family, between team and family and within the team. An outstanding feature of the overlapping interview can be seen in the summary given by the therapist to the oncoming team member. His review not only informs the visiting therapist of the content and progress of the session but also conveys to the patient the therapist's understanding of what the patient feels and thinks.

Some general interpretations can be offered, describing certain family styles, congruencies and incongruencies in a tactful way. The therapist encourages the patient to correct or enlarge the summary thus minimizing any pretense of infallibility. The incoming therapist in turn shares information or impressions gained from other family members. It is essential to keep a careful balance between honesty and tact by selecting information to be shared in a way that it will bridge communication gaps rather than destroy trust in the therapists or create further family splits. The descretion and clinical judgment of the more experienced team member will provide a model for the junior members to follow. In the separate as well as in the overlapping sessions some of the existing resources are explored and plans for further evaluation, planning or treatment begin to emerge.

Final Team-Family Session

Frequently team members conduct a brief conference without the family before the final team-family session. Convergence develops with the integration of information gathered from various sessions, along with the intake data and reports from referring sources, school and family physician. In sharing impressions, feelings and recommendations it is typical for the less experienced team members to be overwhelmed by the overload of information obtained verbally and nonverbally in their contacts with the family. They regularly get "sucked into" the powerful dynamic forces of the family and identify themselves with different members, typically with the symptomatic youth who may be seen as a powerless victim of vicious parental or social forces. Indeed it is not uncommon that the entire team mirrors family dysfunctional interaction until they themselves become aware of it or a supervisor interprets and helps them recognize the pattern. This "gut awareness" is most useful to really understand how the dynamic equilibrium of the family affects all its members. We have to also underline how the index patient contributes through deviant behaviors to the maintenance of the disturbed equilibrium.

Finding ways of negotiating change through family members who are willing to break the now predictable patterns is one of the major tasks of the diagnostic team, as the assessment of their readiness and willingness to change is crucial before moving into family therapy per se. Strengths and weaknesses in the family structure and in the function of its members are more clearly understood. The referral symptoms start making sense. Scapegoating mechanisms are more obvious. Often it becomes evident to key family members that the initial contract in which they brought one individual to be changed is now inappropriate. This awareness evokes feelings of depression and guilt, with family members taking turns at blaming themselves. The significance of historical and environmental factors acquires a better perspective.

I have come to prefer having the team conference in which we discuss diagnostic impressions and management plans in front of the family. We agree with Whitaker (1972) in that with this way we become more tactful and honest. The use of jargon becomes irrelevant and as professionals we are forced to describe pathology with respect and simplicity. I am always impressed with the attentiveness of the family and how they appreciate our sharing with them our feelings and reasoning. I do not think this approach is indicated when the evaluation process is far from reaching closure or when team members have serious divergences that may not be explained merely on countertransferential terms. Teams or small groups have family-like qualities and may be dysfunctional not just because they are replicating or amplifying family pathology. The use of supervisors and consultants minimizes the possible deleterious impact of a "disturbed" team. In our long experience the advantages of the use of teams far outweigh the occasional difficulties because in most cases there is a high degree of convergence among team members.

After participating for over two hours of significant interaction with the team, the family members have typically experienced a new awareness of their difficulties in the climate of respect, honesty, and openness presented to them. The symptoms they brought to our attention have become more understandable and are frequently "owned" by several or by most family members. This does not apply of course to those cases where a key family member suppresses essential information, carries a hidden agenda not uncovered until the end or will engage in dishonest manipulations while intimidating other family members. Then the cautious use of confrontation and interpretation is indicated in order to precipitate a crisis seen of therapeutic value. This requires good timing and considerable self-awareness by the therapist to minimize victimizing family members in a power struggle. A therapist who is unclear about the boundaries of his role and of his authority may misrepresent as therapeutic confrontation what in reality is the acting out of his power fantasies. This session concludes with the planning for further specialized psychiatric, psychological, neurological, psychoeducational and/or further family evaluation. In a large number of cases it is possible to move into a family therapy program and contract for a limited number of team-family therapy sessions—average six to ten spaced weekly or every two weeks for one to one and one-half hours. Frequently we like to combine several individual sessions and/or group therapy and/or placement in our educotherapy program in the overall plan.

A final team debriefing takes place shortly after the family leaves. This serves the purpose of clarification of team interaction, family and individual dynamics with senior consultants including the planning for further diagnostic work, treatment or disposition. Consultants are typically available in all evaluations.

In about 30 percent of the cases seen a pattern offering one or two sessions and including recommendations to other agencies is found adequate. Following the initial team-family evaluation, we see in those cases enough evidence of impact and of self-rehabilitative processes on the way. A follow-up in one to two months is scheduled at which time most often progress has been established and the goals of the family and of the referring source have been met. The team remains available to the family for further consultation as needed.

In about 20 percent of the cases further care and follow-up is handled by the community representatives that functioned as conveners of a family under their care. Typically this involves mental health professionals and paraprofessionals from other centers, school counselors, juvenile officers, clergymen, and welfare workers. In such cases the team-family evaluation has provided consultation and training to the convener in addition to primary care of the family.

MOVING INTO FAMILY THERAPY

When we move from team-family evaluation to a family therapy phase a smaller team is quite adequate and a co-therapy twosome provides a good balance. In most cases the co-therapists participated in the evaluation process, thereby facilitating continuity of care and rapport with the family. Larger teams are needed only where an extended family network is involved. The average course of family therapy involves six to ten sessions, frequently on a weekly basis during the early phase, followed by spacing the meetings every two weeks or more. To help the family experience change and growth by itself dependency must be minimized. Maximum effort to help each family member assume responsibility for personal change must be made, as for instance the designing of homework which will not be controlled by others for its success or failure. This facilitates the redefinition of self-boundaries and the feeling of being in command as individuals. Such experiences frequently break the interlocking dysfunctional equilibrium and open new avenues or more functional interaction and respect between family members. Often the homework looks to them as insignificant, unacceptable or even detrimental to another member of the family. A case in point is the mother who is afraid of disturbing her child who regularly intrudes while she is in the bathroom. Once she decides to experiment locking the door and setting a clear boundary for her privacy, she experiences great relief after some initial distress. The same relief may be experienced by the father who regularly jumps his son as he behaves provocatively toward his mother and later is constantly reprimanded by his wife for not showing love to his son. He chose to experiment, giving himself five minutes before taking the "bait." He reports that he enjoyed the feeling of mastery which he experienced with new understanding and perspective. For the young man who expects his father to deny him privileges and thus presents his requests in anger or with poor timing, awareness of the self-defeating pattern allows him to try as homework to schedule sufficient time with his parents to bargain for permission to take a demanding summer job away from home. He was impressed with how well they listened and responded to the factual information he presented without anger or pressure.

The fact that successes are achieved and "owned" by each member greatly facilitates descapegoating and stops the mutual blaming which tends to slow down or arrest the natural growth potential of a stable and functional family system.

Let me emphasize again the need for flexibility which in the context of a family-centered treatment program makes it possible to include individual therapy for one or more members, medication, group therapy, a referral for special education placement, vocational rehabilitation, day care or residential treatment.

As their defensive patterns are mobilized, families frequently experience more discomfort and present resistance to further intervention. They may close ranks defending themselves and perceiving the team as an enemy. Other times they may try to seduce the therapists with premature leaps into health (Zuk, 1971). The family is experiencing new awareness that brings out fear, excitement, sadness, anger, confusion and ultimate joy. Respect in their strengths conveyed by the team allows them to unfold their healthy resources while recognizing what is pathological and dysfunctional. Redefinition of roles and clarification of generational boundaries, of patterns of interaction and of communication also facilitates a rapid process of self-rehabilitation.

Long-term team-family therapy is, in our experience as an outpatient program, less feasible because of the time commitment required from family members and because of other clinical considerations. When indicated it involves a seriously disturbed member, typically a psychotic or borderline psychotic youth which requires treatment over an extended period of time. In most cases, we maintain a family-centered orientation focusing on one or two of the more available family members in individual, conjoint or group therapy including occasional sessions with the whole family particularly at the time of crises, extended vacations or termination.

TERMINATION

Termination is planned from the very first as treatment goals are established and strengths are assessed. It has been our experience that working through is done by the family members in the real world and not in the therapist's office. Because dependency is not fostered, families learn to rely on their own strengths. I do not want to convey the impression that family therapy solves all mental health troubles. "Thinking family" provides an excellent perspective of the pathological and of the healthy forces in the ecosystem of individuals. Proficiency in other treatment modalities by the therapists is a must as well as knowledge of existing community resources. Training should also provide for the healthy recognition that some families unwilling to change are untreatable. However, even in those cases a family orientation can be used to minimize the negative impact of a chaotic or an oppressive family by carefully developing and maintaining a therapeutic alliance with key members while a more individualized treatment approach is offered to those willing to change.

We find that team-family therapy makes the termination process easier. Perhaps it is less conflicting for families to leave the therapist when he is not alone, not unlike the adolescent experiencing less conflict if he goes away from home leaving two parents that have a good relationship to support each other.

Family Therapy with Adolescents

Another application of co-therapy answers the argument frequently used to avoid involving the adolescents with their families. The reasoning explains that developmentally the adolescent tries to separate himself from the family, sharpens his sense of identity and moves away from them physically and emotionally. We find that most of the adolescents who come to our attention have unclear self-boundaries. Family assessment and family treatment helps them clarify these boundaries and often redefines their identity in the context of their family. The use of a team provides more neutral areas for the adolescent and his family to relate to. Frequently one of the therapists may then be more polarized in the direction of the parents while another is able to develop a closer understanding of the adolescent. It is also possible to split the family to provide separate interviews at one time or another for different members including siblings and members of the extended family.

SOME FINAL THOUGHTS

We find it most helpful to think in terms of ecological social systems within the format of the team-family-centered technology. The complexities of understanding emotional, behavioral and learning disorders cannot be explained by one simple theoretical model, or etiology. It is unlikely that one professional will ever have all the knowledge and the technical expertise needed to integrate all the items of information surrounding the presenting symptoms. The traditional use of an orthopsychiatric team studying a case separately, frequently fails to integrate theoretical concepts or to explain how disturbed symptoms emerge. To study those symptoms in isolation is to ignore that they appear in a social framework and that they are only relevant in the ecological context in which they appear. The team-family model offers us an ideal approach to the evaluation and the treatment of emotional disorders with an ecological systems philosophy.

These current adaptations of the multiple impact therapy approach also facilitate the use of wider treatment possibilities, notably combining therapies to include individual, couples, group, family and network techniques in as much as the therapists do not need to participate conjointly in all treatment modalities.

A most useful aspect in the use of team-family therapy relates to the ease with which additional professionals and trainees can become members of the team (Serrano, 1973). We regularly incorporate medical students during their brief psychiatric clerkship to get exposed to the ecological aspects of mental and emotional illness. Their rotation has consistently been reported as one of the most exciting and relevant psychiatric learning experiences they had. Quoting a recent graduate "that is where psychiatry is at."

REFERENCES

Ackerman, N.W.: *The Psychodynamics of Family Life: Diagnosis and Treatment of Family Relationships.* New York, Basic Books, 1958.

Auerswald, E.H.: Interdisciplinary versus ecological approach. In Sager and Kaplan (Eds.): *Progress in Group and Family Therapy,* New York, Brunner and Mazel, 1972, pp. 309-321.

Caplan, G.: An approach to the study of the family mental health. *Public Health Rep,* 71:1027-1030, 1956.

Johnson, A.M.: Collaborative psychotherapy: team setting. In Heiman, M. (Ed.): *Psychoanalysis and Social Work.* New York, International University Press, 1953.

MacGregor, R., Ritchie, A.M., Serrano, A.C., Schuster, F.P., Goolishian, H.A., and McDanald, E.C.: *Multiple Impact Therapy.* New York, McGraw-Hill Book Co., 1964.

Peck, H.B.: An application of group therapy to the intake process. *Am J Orthopsychiatry,* 23:338-349, 1953.

Serrano, A.C.: *Multiple Therapy.* Unpublished manuscript, 1973.

Whitaker, C., and Napier, A.: A conversation about co-therapy. In Farber, Mendelshon, and Napier (Eds.): *The Book of Family Therapy.* New York, Science House, 1972, pp. 480-506.

Whitaker, C., Warkentin, H., and Johnson, N.L.: A philosophical basis for brief psychotherapy. *Psychiat Q,* 23:439-443, 1949.

Zuk, G.H.: *Family Therapy: A Triadic-based Approach.* New York, Behavioral Publications, 1971, pp. 43-82.

INDEX

A

Ackerman, N.W., 159, 172
Adult education courses, 40
Alimony, 139
American Association of Marriage and
  Family Counselors, 9
American Psychological Association, 9
Ansell, Charles, v, 51
Auerswald, E.H., 160, 172
Axline, V., 122

B

Beebe, J., 157
Biller, H., 101, 122
Bohannan, Paul, 17, 29
Bowlby, J., 91, 114, 122

C

Caplan, Gerald, 159, 172
Church, J., 102, 122
Computer dating service, 45
Confidentiality, 8
Conquering Loneliness, 48
Counseling, 4
  crisis intervention, 125
  educative, 27
  group, 48, 142, 150, 153
  individual, 149, 153
  marital, 3, 4, 124
  role, 28
Crisis intervention counseling, 125
Cull, John G., v, 3, 142

D

Dahms, Alan M., 28, 29
Despert, L., 95, 122
Deutsch, H., 114, 122, 166
Divorce, 6, 31
  counselors, 31, 50
  men, 51
  no-fault, 31

parents, 93, 106
proceedings, 51
settlement, 72
situations, 40
trauma, 121
women, 15, 65, 85

E

Educative counseling, 27
Ellis, Albert, 49
Emerson, James G., 11, 29
Emotional
  preparation, 54
  reactions, 13
  upheaval, 13
Empathic understanding, 6
Extramarital sexual activity, 17

F

Family
  crisis, 95
  dissolution, 102
  structure, 121
  therapy, 167
Fenichel, O., 122
Flavell, J., 104, 122
Frankl, Viktor E., 23, 29
Free association, 156
Fromm, Erich, 11, 29

G

Gendlin, E.T., 154, 157
Goldman, George D., 14, 29
Goode, W.J., 25, 29
Goodman, David, 16, 29
Goolishian, H.A., 172
Grief, 21
Group
  leader, 152
  marital therapy, 142, 150, 153